# GCSE
## English Exam Techniques

*a 15-week revision programme*

**Authors:**

**Keith Brindle,**
Assistant Principal Examiner, NEAB

**John Nield,**
Principal Examiner, NEAB

# Introduction

Your questions answered.

**Q: What is the point of this book?**
   A: The aims of this book are:

- to give a **clear insight** into the skills you need to succeed in GCSE English exams
- to show **when** and **where** those skills need to be demonstrated
- to **practise** those skills, and give the opportunity to **develop** them **on your own**
- to **explain** how your **work is marked** by examiners
- to **provide** a **structured programme** that leads right up to the exams themselves

and, most important of all,

- to **enable you to gain those extra marks** which will improve your chance of **a higher grade.**

**Q: But you can't revise English, can you?**
   A: English may not appear to be a subject with lots of facts, figures or formulae, but, like any other subject, it has component parts and skills that can be practised and learned. This book has a series of structured units which will focus on those parts and skills.

**Q: How can this book help me get a better grade, then?**
   A: You should work through the book, unit by unit. However, if this is not possible, you can focus on key pages or sections which you – or your teacher – consider to be problematic. As you will see, the book has a clear structure which is easy to follow.

**Q: So, how is this revision book structured?**
   A: There are 15 units (including a final checklist) – which could fit the 15 weeks before your exam. Each one deals with a key aspect of the English exam, whether it's 'Knowing the Papers' or 'Writing to Argue'. Each Unit is between 4–6 pages long and is split into 4 sections:

- the opening section gives **advice** and **information**
- the second section gives **practice**, often in small 'bite-size' chunks
- the third section gives **further practice**, with more developed writing
- the final section provides **extension work** and shows you **how to move up a grade**, using key skills that you, yourself, identify.

**Q: Is there anything else to help me?**
   A: Yes. On many pages, we, the authors of this book (two senior examiners with NEAB, the Board who set your exam), offer **Examiner's Tips** – that is, key pointers to improve your work. Also, each Unit ends with a **summary** of the main points covered.

**Q: Sounds great. When can I get started?**
   A: That's easy – just turn the page.

Keith Brindle, John Nield

# Contents

| Unit 1 | Knowing the Papers | 4 |
| Unit 2 | Reading Non-Literary Texts | 8 |
| Unit 3 | Comparing Non-Literary Texts | 14 |
| Unit 4 | Revising Reading Skills | 20 |
| Unit 5 | Genres | 24 |
| Unit 6 | A Writing Process for Section B | 28 |
| Unit 7 | Revising Writing Skills | 34 |
| Unit 8 | Writing to Argue | 38 |
| Unit 9 | Writing to Persuade | 44 |
| Unit 10 | Writing to Instruct | 50 |
| Unit 11 | Writing to Inform | 56 |
| Unit 12 | Writing to Explain | 60 |
| Unit 13 | Writing to Describe | 64 |
| Unit 14 | Final Revision for English | 68 |
| Unit 15 | Your Final Check List | 72 |

# Unit 1  Knowing the Papers

*Targets*
1. To understand the form of the examination.
2. To know what is tested in English Paper 1.
3. To know what is tested in English Paper 2.

## General Information

The NEAB's English examination has more candidates than any other in the country. It is important, therefore, that you are well prepared: you have a great deal of competition!

### English GCSE  *details*

Coursework:    40% of final mark    20% for written coursework
                                    20% for Speaking and Listening

Examinations:  60% of final mark    30% for Paper 1
                                    30% for Paper 2

Both papers last two hours.

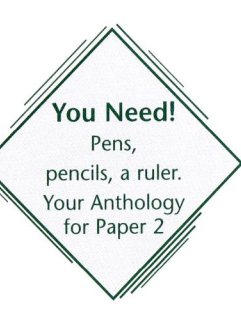

**You Need!** Pens, pencils, a ruler. Your Anthology for Paper 2

The English Literature examination, for which you might also be entered, has one paper lasting two hours. English Literature is a separate subject and receives a separate grade.

In this book, we will be dealing exclusively with the English examination.

**What you need for your English examinations**

Pens, pencils, a ruler.
Your Anthology for Paper 2.

Dictionaries are not allowed.

Of course, it is not enough simply to arrive on the day of the examination with the correct equipment.

You will be tested on a range of skills and, to do well, you need to be aware of:
- what is being tested
- what the examiner is looking for
- and how to produce the best answers.

It is vital that you walk into each examination knowing exactly what is expected of you and confident that you can deal with the questions.

# English Paper 1

- Lasts for two hours.
- Contains two sections, both marked out of 54.
- You should spend about an hour on each section.

## Section A

Section A requires you to write about two or three non-literary texts (i.e. not from novels or poems), which will be printed on the paper. There will be one question, broken into three or four different parts. Answer all parts of the question.

Your reading skills are being tested, to see if you can:
- *tell the difference between fact and opinion*
- *follow an argument through a piece of writing*
- *explain how different texts deal in different ways with the same subject*
- *choose parts of the texts to support your answers*
- *understand why texts are presented in different ways*
- *understand how language is used by different writers.*

**FACTS**
- Time
- Marks

**FOCUS**
Non-Literary Texts
Testing Reading Skills

**A likely pattern for the questions is:**

Question 1 (a)
You will be asked about one of the texts and must select and write about parts of it.
This could involve listing facts or opinions; or explaining certain information.

Question 1 (b)
This question will probably look at another passage.
You might have to explain information or show you can follow an argument.
You are likely to have to answer in full sentences.

Question 1 (c)
You will probably have to compare the two texts you have read, their purposes, layout and presentation, and language.
You are likely to be asked which text is more successful in what it sets out to do.

There are 54 marks in Section A: see how many marks are available for each part of the question and spend a minute for each mark. If 5 marks are available, spend 5 minutes on that part of the question.

Minutes = Marks
**EXAMINER'S TIP!**

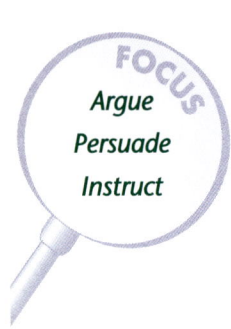

### Section B

Section B requires you to write about a subject that has some connection with the texts used in Section A. You choose one question to answer. You will have to:
- **argue** (Question 2)
- **persuade** (Question 3)

or
- **instruct** (Question 4).

**FOCUS**
Argue
Persuade
Instruct

Your writing skills are being tested and you will be marked on your:
- *content: the ideas and information you include*
- *ability to write for a given audience and purpose*
- *ability to organise writing, so that what you say flows effectively and logically*
- *paragraphing*
- *accuracy: sentences, spelling and expression.*

You are advised to write about **two sides**. Spend:
- **10** minutes planning
- **40** minutes writing
- **10** minutes checking.

## English Paper 2

**FACTS**
- Time
- Marks

- Lasts for two hours.
- Contains two sections, both marked out of 54.
- You should spend about one hour on each section.

### Section A

All questions are related to the **Anthology.** Bring it with you to the examination. Your school is unlikely to have spare copies.

Your Anthology can contain brief annotations, but you must not write sentences in it.

**FOCUS**
Anthology

Your reading skills are being tested, and in your answers you will be expected to:
- *respond to the poems*
- *explain what they are saying*
- *use appropriate parts of the poems to explain your points*
- *compare and contrast poems*
- *write about the language, how poems are presented on the page and how they are constructed*
- *comment on the way language is used differently in the poems.*

You will be asked about what the poems have to say and how they say it.

Unit 1  Knowing the Papers

**Section A has two parts:**

For each part, you must write about **at least two poems** in your answer.

**Part 1: Poets**
- Spend 30 minutes writing about **one poet**, chosen from the three in Part 1 of the Anthology.
- Choose **one** of the two questions offered.

**Part 2: Poems from Other Cultures and Traditions**
- Spend 30 minutes writing about two **'Poems from other Cultures and Traditions'**.
- Again, choose **one** question.

## Section B

This section tests the same writing skills as Section B in Paper 1. Choose **one** question and write about **two** sides. You must write to:

- **inform** (Question 2)
- **explain** (Question 3)

or

- **describe** (Question 4).

Spend:
- **10** minutes planning
- **40** minutes writing
- **10** minutes checking.

*Planning*

*Writing*

*Checking*

FOCUS
Inform
Explain
Describe

Check | Plan | Write

Finally, re-read this Unit, then working in pairs test each other.

# Knowing the Papers

### How much have you remembered?

1. Which examination paper involves the Anthology?
2. How many poems from Other Cultures and Traditions will you have to write about?
3. What kinds of essays will be expected from you in English Paper 1?
4. In English Paper 1, Section A, how many texts are you likely to have to read?
5. If, in Paper 1, Section A, a question carries 20 marks, how long should you spend answering it?
6. How many poets will you write about in Paper 2, Section A, Part 1?
7. What are you allowed to write inside your Anthology?
8. How should you divide up the time available to write essays in Section B?
9. When comparing texts in Paper 1, Section A, what aspects of the texts will you be concentrating on?
10. How many marks are available for each section of both papers?

# Unit 2  Reading Non-Literary Texts

*Targets*

To learn about Paper 1, Section A:
1. To learn what is tested.
2. To learn how to respond to the questions.

Section A of Paper 1 requires you to examine two or three non-literary texts: these could be newspaper articles; magazine articles or leaflets; biographies or autobiographies; letters; advertisements; diary entries or obituaries.

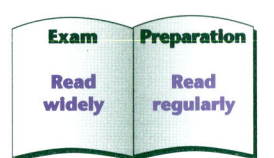

To prepare for this examination, you must read widely and regularly!

There will probably be one question on each text, and a final question which asks you to compare two of the texts. This unit deals with the initial questions on individual texts; comparisons will be dealt with in Unit 3 (page 14).

**Exam Preparation**
Read widely
Read regularly

### What is tested in the initial questions?

The style of questions varies slightly from year to year, however, you will almost certainly be expected to write about:

- **facts** in the texts: things that are certain, that can be proved, that have happened or that exist beyond any doubt
- **opinions** – people's views or beliefs, their interpretations of events, how they see things, what someone considers to be the truth.

You will be expected to be able to:

- **follow an argument** – read through the text and decide what it is saying
- **select appropriate material** – put relevant points into answers and sometimes quote words, phrases or sentences.

It is vital that you read the questions carefully. Underline or highlight the most important words, so you concentrate on what is required:

e.g. 'What do we learn about the history of foxhunting?'
'Explain, in your own words, the writer's opinion of football supporters.'

**Read Questions Carefully!**
**EXAMINER'S TIP!**

Read this newspaper report.

**PRACTICE**

# Offenders reformed by victims

## New method proves effective in changing criminals' lives

The Home Office recently released details of an experiment which has brought together young offenders and their victims. The face-to-face meetings have been producing remarkable results.

Statistics show that most young offenders re-offend within two years. Incredibly, the figure can be as high as 89% for 15 and 16 year olds. This is a situation which has been allowed to continue for years because there has been no system in place, to change the ways of the criminals. Imprisonment punishes them, but does not make them reform their ways.

However, the Leeds Probation Service has been trialling a new approach. Victim and offender sit down together, and the victim learns why the offender committed the crime.

More importantly, the offender has to take responsibility for what he has done. Put simply: the offenders, when they have to listen to the sufferings of the victims, realise the errors of their ways. They get to know the real person they have hurt. PC Dove, a peacemaking mediator, says: "You can turn someone's life around. Often, these are not bad young people; they simply did a bad thing."

PC Dove and those working with him seem to have a point: 68% of youngsters involved in the project had not re-offended after two years. One boy summed up what had happened to him: "My life's changed 'cos I made it change." And that seems to sum up the success of the venture.

*facts*

### Task 1

What details in the report prove that the scheme has been successful?

(3 marks)

The important words are <u>details</u>, <u>prove</u> and <u>successful</u>.
'Prove' must be related to **facts**. Here, the *statistics* help prove the writer's point.
Write down **three facts** to answer this question.

## Task 2

**opinions**

What does the writer think was wrong with the old system and why does he believe the new one is more successful? (3 marks)

The important words are <u>thinks</u> ... <u>wrong with the old system</u>, and <u>why</u> ... <u>believe ... new one is more successful</u>.

This is a more difficult question: it has two parts and we are considering **opinions**.

You must read the article carefully; to **follow the argument**, then **select the appropriate details**.

Find and explain **four things** that were wrong with the old system, according to the writer; and **four reasons** given to show the new one is better.

### PRACTICE

**How to get Marks!**

**Consider the mark scheme.**

For Task 1, you should have mentioned the following:
- 'Statistics show that most young offenders re-offend within two years' and
- 'the figure can be as high as 89% for 15 and 16 year olds'
- but '68% of youngsters involved in the project had not re-offended after two years'.

(3 marks)

For Task 2, you might have included the following:
- figures for re-offending have been too high ("incredibly")
- there has been no system to change criminals' ways
- prison only punishes criminals
- it does not reform them

but

- figures suggest the new system works better
- offenders have to realise they have hurt a real person
- and have to accept what they have done is wrong
- people's lives can be changed.

(8 marks)

**EXAMINER'S TIP!** 8 marks = 8 points & 8 minutes spent

Always notice the number of marks available for each question or part-question. When you are finding information, they indicate how many points you should make in your answer; and approximately how many minutes to spend on it.

### Task 3

Mark your answers.

### Task 4

**If you missed any of the points, check back and see where they came from.**

Ensure that if you were asked the questions again you would get them right.

*Mark Check Test*

### Task 5

Test yourself.

Choose any newspaper or magazine article of a similar length to the one on page 9. Make a note of how facts, opinions and arguments are used, as in the example below.

## Fake Lord Fools Americans

A new way of stitching up rich visitors from across the pond was uncovered yesterday at Wyndelbury Manor, the home of Lord Wacket of Wyndelbury. A distant relative, Sheryl Tucker, from Tucson, Arizona suddenly realised during a £400-a-head banquet that the aristocrat whose grand country house she had paid an over-priced £2000 to stay in was not in fact Lord Wacket, but an actor, Timothy Dalford, employed to play the part of Lord Wacket during the holiday season.

*Timothy Dalford*

A probe of other country houses in the area has revealed that over 40% run scams along similar lines.

**My Notes**

*facts:*
£400-a-head banquet
she paid £2000
actor played part

*opinions:*
country houses run 'scams'
stay 'overpriced'

Unit 2 Reading Non-Literary Texts

**Shaping for Grading**
**EXAMINER'S TIP!**

To gain better grades, it is not enough just to find the correct information – you are expected to 'use' the details you find, to write convincing answers. It is what examiners call 'shaping' the material.

**FOCUS**
**Shaping**

'Shaping' means:
- explaining what you have found
- moving away from just setting out the points in the order they appear in the text
- writing about them, rather than just listing them.

## Extension Work: Shaping

Re-read the article on page 9.

Question: Explain how the writer tries to persuade us that the new system is an improvement.

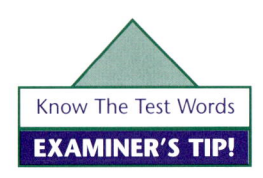

**Know The Test Words**
**EXAMINER'S TIP!**

'Explain', like 'In your own words', means you should not just be copying. When you explain, you make sense of something for the reader.

### Task 6

**three opening answers by candidates in the exam:**

---

**F Grade**
*The writer tells us it is better. Face to face meetings have been producing results. Usually young offenders re-offend within two years. As high as 89%. When they sit down together, the victim learns why the criminal committed the crime and the offender has to take responsibility for what he has done …*

**C Grade**
*The writer uses facts and opinions to persuade us that the new system is better. He says that 89% of 15 and 16 year olds usually re-offend within two years, and in his opinion the old system has done nothing to change them whilst they have been in prison. However, the Leeds Probation Service makes the victim and the offender sit down together and the writer thinks that has made a difference because the criminals start to see that they have done wrong …*

---

Unit 2 Reading Non-Literary Texts

**A\* Grade**
*Even in the title, the writer is exerting influence on us so we believe that the new system is an improvement. 'Offenders reformed' and 'proves effective' clearly indicate his opinion. Later, he sensibly compares the old statistics, which show that as many as 89% of 15 and 16 year olds re-offend almost immediately, with the figures from Leeds, which show that 68% of young offenders in the project have stayed out of trouble for at least two years. He tells us how the new project works and quotes the aptly-named PC Dove …*

## Task 7

**Write responses to the following:**

**a)** Look at the 'F Grade' response and the article itself. Is the candidate explaining the writer's technique? What has the candidate done with the information in the passage?

**b)** Why is the 'C Grade' response better?

**c)** Say why the final extract is the best. Look at:

- how the candidate deals with facts and opinions
- how the candidate puts details into a different order to make a point
- how words or phrases show the candidate is responding to the material, rather than just saying what is in it (e.g. 'he sensibly compares').

*FOCUS: Comparing Grades*

## Task 8

**Continue the A\* response, using the skills you have just identified.**

*Examiner's Summary*

- Read widely, to develop your understanding and skills, and practise on other texts.
- Expect to have to write about facts and opinions.
- Answer the question that has been set and notice how many marks are available.
- On the Higher Tier, aim to *shape* your writing unless you are told to list details.

# Unit 3   Comparing Non-Literary Texts

**Targets**

**To learn how to:**

1. Read the question carefully.
2. Make brief notes for each bullet point, referring to both texts.
3. Find proof for your points and employ technical terms.
4. Write effectively, explaining the material and its effects.

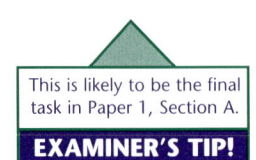

**EXAMINER'S TIP!** This is likely to be the final task in Paper 1, Section A.

See Unit 1 page 5 for more information

| | | |
|---|---|---|
| Read carefully | *means* | check the main requirement of the question, then what the bullet points require. |
| Make brief notes | *means* | write a quick plan, using the bullet points as sub-headings. |
| Find proof for your points | *means* | include in your plan short quotations from the texts as evidence, and use technical terms you have learnt. |
| Develop your points | *means* | explain details, don't just list them. |

### Stage 1: Read the question carefully

The bullet points lead you through a comparison of the texts. You might be asked

- to write about **content**, **language**, **facts** and **opinions**, **layout** and **presentation**, and the **success** of the texts

or

- to **focus** on just **some of these elements.**

### Stage 2: Make brief notes

- Do this quickly.
- Organise notes using the bullets as sub-headings.
- Cover all bullet points and both texts.
- Make your notes precise and detailed.

## Stage 3: Find proof and use technical terms

Do not copy out long quotations. Highlight or underline the quotations you need on the texts and make a brief reference to them in your plan.

Choose some technical terms which fit the texts you are looking at. For example: *factual, opinion, subjective, objective, rhetorical, emotive, irony, metaphor, simile, alliteration, headline, italics, etc.* See Unit 4 (page 22) for a more detailed list.

**FOCUS: Comparing Texts**

## Stage 4: Write your answer, developing your points

- Do not simply copy out your plan. Discuss points of layout or language, saying why the writer has used them and whether they are effective.
- Do not forget you are comparing the two texts and judging them against each other.

Read the newspaper report below.

**PRACTICE**

### Students bored to breaking point

"I just said what everyone else was thinking," says student excluded for speaking out.

Is it time our outdated approaches to schooling came into line with the modern world? That is the question being debated in a small town in the Midlands after a fifteen-year-old pupil was excluded from school for saying he found assembly boring.

Elliott: "I'm no troublemaker."

Elliott Byron had never been in serious trouble throughout his life at Durnhill High School in Barton, Warwickshire, until he dared to write to the local paper, complaining about his headteacher's assemblies. Then he was suspended.

"I come to school to learn, not to be bored every morning," said Elliott. And, despite the fact that most children feel the same way about assembly, Mrs Garland, his headteacher, was not amused.

Elliott is unrepentant: "I'm only saying what the others say. But the teachers are treating me like a bully or a vandal. I thought we had the right to speak out in this country. The other children say I'm a hero now, so I'm not going to say sorry. Why should I?"

Unit 3  *Comparing Non-Literary Texts*  15

**Now read this autobiographical extract:**

## From 'My Way' by David Sampson

I eventually gave up teaching because I found that, increasingly, the pupils were becoming like their parents. They challenged everything I said and believed they had the right to do as they wished. I have always believed that a child is in school to be taught and to be made into a future citizen of a country of which we should all be proud. Yet, if the adults behave with no consideration for others and their children learn that way of thinking from them, what hope is there for the poor teachers?

Schools need to be given more power over their pupils. They need to be supported by the government. They need to be supported by the police. They need to be compulsory and must take place. There should be more emphasis on Religious Education. We have turned into a society with no faith in God and no interest in others. Unless we act quickly to turn the tide, we could find that there is no way back to decency and the belief that the world can be a better place.

### Task 1

Make notes on the following question:

Compare the two extracts. In your answer, discuss:

- the layout of each extract
- the use made of facts and opinions
- how the language tries to capture our interest
- what the writers think about schools, assemblies and the rights of children
- which extract persuades us most successfully.

Unit 3 *Comparing Non-Literary Texts*

Your notes on 'Students bored to breaking point' should look something like this:

| | |
|---|---|
| **Layout** | • headline   • sub-heading<br>• columns   • photograph<br>• short, journalistic, paragraphs |
| **Facts** | • excluded for saying assembly boring<br>• letter to paper criticised head's assemblies |
| **Opinions** | • kind of child Elliott is said to be<br>• what the writer chooses to quote from Elliott<br>• writer's phrasing: 'dared', 'most children feel the same', 'Garland not amused', etc. |
| **Language** | • newspaper style (sentences begin with 'And' and 'But')<br>• alliteration in headings ('bored to breaking point'; 'suspended for speaking')<br>• use of quotation: generally subjective report<br>• simile ('like a bully or a vandal')<br>• metaphor ('I'm a hero')<br>• rhetorical questions ('Why should I?') |
| **What the writer thinks** | • suggests approaches 'outdated'<br>• Elliott brave to oppose assemblies ('dared')<br>• only Elliott quoted ('I'm no troublemaker')<br>• says others agree with Elliott: opinion given without proof<br>• picture chosen to make Elliott seem cheerful and respectable |
| **Success** | • easy to follow<br>• sense that one student is bravely standing against the school system<br>• fight is being waged by someone who 'is not a troublemaker' |

### Task 2

Develop your first set of notes on the article 'My Way', so they are as detailed as the ones above.

You can examine non-literary texts by using the headings above whenever you read. The more you practise, the quicker you will be able to do it!

**Practise These Headings**
**EXAMINER'S TIP!**

### Task 3

Now write a full answer to the original question in essay style, comparing the two texts and using the two sets of notes.

Unit 3   Comparing Non-Literary Texts

**Go For Better Grades!**

# Extension Work: Assessing your response

**Task 4**

Apply this mark scheme to your work and decide which grade description your work is closest to.

---

**F Grade**

You

- concentrated on just one text
- mentioned layout/presentation, by saying that there is a picture, or columns or headings
- said the writers use facts and opinions to convince us (you might have selected one or two)
- said something about the language, perhaps that it is hard to understand, or easy
- said what the extracts are about
- said which one you liked best.


**C Grade**

You

- dealt with both texts
- mentioned various aspects of layout/presentation, saying how they affect the reader (e.g. 'This draws our attention to …')
- picked out facts and opinions, saying what the writer intended (e.g. 'Elliott is made to seem …')
- quoted words or phrases, saying how they affect the reader (e.g. 'This makes us think that …')
- showed the differences in the writers' opinions
- assessed their success, bearing in mind the things you had already discussed in the answer.


**A Grade**

You

- were able to consider and compare both texts throughout
- discussed layout/presentation and language, tying your comments to the writers' intentions (e.g.'Because the writer wants everyone to feel sorry for Elliott, he …'; 'In contrast, the second writer is appealing to a more intellectual audience, so he …')
- commented precisely and in detail on layout/presentation and language (e.g. 'These short sentences use a repetitive structure to build to a climax …')
- discussed the balance between fact and opinion and how the reader is persuaded by the mixture
- assessed the writers' views, blending your comments into an assessment of how successful each was, but using your own phrases and sentence structures (e.g. 'David Sampson's subjective analysis of the situation convinces the reader because he allows no room for argument. The paragraphs themselves seem solid like building blocks …').

## Task 5

If your answer did not merit an A Grade, try again, using the mark scheme to guide your efforts.

*Examiner's Summary*

- This question carries many marks.

- Spend as many minutes on it as there are marks awarded.

- Respond to each bullet point.

- Answer in detail, and explain effects; don't just repeat the same information contained in the exam passages.

- Prepare for the question by examining non-literary texts before the examination, looking for features highlighted in this unit.

# Good comparison = good grades

# Unit 4  Revising Reading Skills

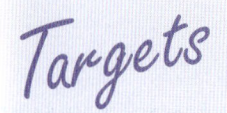

*Targets*

In order to read effectively and follow an argument you will need:

1. To locate facts and recognise opinions.
2. To answer questions precisely.
3. To quote appropriately.
4. To explain clearly.
5. To use a technical vocabulary.
6. To write at an appropriate length.

### Skill 1: Locating facts and recognising opinions

A fact is a fixed piece of information, that is beyond dispute, and can be proved; an opinion is a belief that cannot be completely measured or proved.

Examples:

**Fact:** English is a subject taught in schools

**Opinion:** All English teachers are beautiful

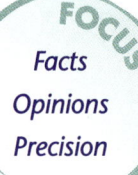

*FOCUS*
*Facts*
*Opinions*
*Precision*

**Task 1**

Read the following extract then write down five facts and five opinions:

London is the capital of Great Britain. It lures tourists from around the world because it is famous for its historical past, its buildings and the welcome it gives: it has Buckingham Palace, the Houses of Parliament, Big Ben and Trafalgar Square. More recently, it has become well known for hosting the largest marathon in Great Britain and for the Millennium Dome. Three words sum up the London experience; history, heritage and hospitality.

### Skill 2: Answering questions precisely

You are expected to read questions accurately and to give the information that is asked for. As in the example below, underline or highlight key words on the question paper.

What <u>impression</u> of London is the writer trying to create? How does he <u>use</u> <u>facts</u> and <u>opinions</u> to create the impression?

### Task 2

Now write about:
- what sort of facts he chooses and why (does he write about night life? shopping?)
- what sort of phrasing he uses to put across his opinion and the effect he is seeking.

### Remember!

| ● Don't simply list facts and opinions. | ● Write about the mood the writer wants the reader to experience. | ● Show how he blends facts and opinions to promote that feeling. |
|---|---|---|

## Skill 3: Quoting appropriately

- Quotations should be brief, appropriate and necessary.
- They should be placed in quotation marks.
- If longer than three words, they should be written on a new line.
- They usually come after a point you make, as a way of proving it.

**FOCUS**
Quotations
Alliteration

### Task 3

How does the writer use alliteration at the end of the passage?

Explain the effect of the words 'history, heritage and hospitality', then quote it. Start with 'The writer uses alliteration in the final sentence in order to ...'

## Skill 4: Explaining clearly

This will save time, avoid confusion and collect marks.

Read the following confusing sentences:

1. 'He says that when something is thrown across the class even if it is a girl, a boy gets the blame.'

2. 'They went driving for a while and hoped to bump into their friend.'

3. 'When the disease broke out, they closed the school because they had to catch it early.'

**Explaining clearly will:**
- save time
- avoid confusion
- collect marks

### Task 4

Write down what the writers intended to say, and what each sentence actually suggests.

**21**

Unit 4 Revising Reading Skills

### Skill 5: Using a technical vocabulary

You could not talk about a tennis match without using words like 'net', 'serve', 'set' and so on. In the same way, you need the correct words to comment precisely on texts.

Look at these words. Do you know what each means?

**Style/language:**

Standard English, conversational, formal, argumentative, persuasive, factual, opinionated, informative, patronising, journalistic, subjective, objective, facts, figures, metaphors, similes, alliteration, onomatopoeia, emotive, rhetorical, repetition, quotation.

**Presentation/layout**

bullet-points, columns, headings, sub-headings, illustrations, diagrams, italics, bold print, font, justified, centred, logos, icons, symbols, headlines, margin, by-line, indent, photographs, prose, verse.

**Use:** a dictionary or ask a teacher

### Task 5

a) Select three words you do not understand and find out what they mean.
b) Write three sentences, using one of the words in each, to show you can use them effectively.

E.g. *The way the politician dealt with the teenage protester was very patronising, when he said she had done her best but should leave politics to 'grown-ups'.*

**Terms Mean Top Grades**
**EXAMINER'S TIP!**

Revise technical terms, such as the ones in the list above, the night before English Paper 1. Used correctly, they will impress the examiner.

### Skill 6: Writing at an appropriate length

- Always check how many marks are available for a question or part-question.

- This information is clearly presented at the right-hand side of the paper, beside the question.

- As a general rule, you should spend as many minutes on each question as there are marks for it. There are 54 marks available for Paper 1, Section A. As you have an hour to answer, spending 54 minutes answering the question, worth 54 marks, will allow you 6 minutes for reading and checking your work.

# Extension Work: Writing about the success of texts

Having examined two or more texts in Section A of Paper 1, you might be asked:
- which is the most successful

or
- which writer puts across a message most effectively.

The best answers discuss the purpose of a text and judge the effectiveness of its:
- language
- presentation and layout.

**FOCUS: Successful Texts**

The answer becomes a blend of the skills we have been practising.

Read these three conclusions to a comparison question based on two articles about old people. Each conclusion is by a different student.

### Extract 1 (Grade F):
*I thought the writer was boring all the way through the article. She didn't tell me anything I wanted to know and I don't think anyone else would be interested unless they were very old. I like to read things that are full of life and about what young people are thinking.*

### Extract 2 (Grade C):
*The writer used language really effectively and made you think about the subject. The way she used headings drew your attention to the different parts of her argument. She had set out to inform the reader about the problems facing old people and did it very well. I am sure that her approach will have won over many young people, because she did not talk down at them.*

### Extract 3 (Grade A):
*Since the writer was attempting to convince young people that the old need our help, she made her article suitably appealing. The three columns represented the three strands of her argument; she varied her style, to capture the way youngsters talk; and she brought to life the dilemmas for old people without ever sounding patronising. Young people can empathise with the old if they are not made to feel guilty. This writer clearly understood how to influence her readers.*

## Task 6

a) Why would Extract 2 be awarded a higher grade than Extract 1?
b) List the qualities of Extract 3 which you cannot find in the other two.

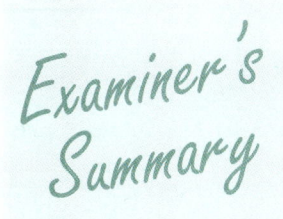

### Examiner's Summary
- Regularly read a range of non-fiction texts before the exam.
- Read the question carefully and do what it asks.
- Unless you are asked to list information, try to analyse text, rather than just repeating what it says.
- Always check how many marks are available for each question and spend the right amount of time on it.

# Unit 5  Genres

**Targets**  To focus on how to write for different purposes and audiences through the use of appropriate:
1. layouts
2. styles of writing/language.

### Paper 1, Section A

For this section you must:
- **recognise** these genres
- **show how layout** and **language** are **used**.

### Paper 1, Section B

For this section you must:
- **produce** writing in **specified genres.**

During lessons, you will have come across many different genres – that is, types of text. The following two key elements are vital in recognising, and writing in different genres.

## Element 1  Layout

Make sure you consider the different elements of presentation, such as:
- columns
- headlines
- sub-headings
- photographs
- illustrations
- boxes
- different paragraph lengths
- italics
- bold type
- various fonts
- letter format

and so on.

You must know **how** and **when** to use these devices.

## Element 2  Style/Language

Depending on topic, purpose and audience, be aware that style can vary. It can be:
- formal or informal
- instructive
- personal
- factual
- reflective
- informative
- persuasive
- technical
- and many, many more.

You must **recognise** different styles and be able to **reproduce** them.

Together, these two elements make the genre. For example, personal writing, presented in chronological day-by-day sequence, in continuous prose = diary.

## Layout

**Task 1**

Read the three blocks of text below.

**Riding bikes can be dangerous:**
- traffic does not leave enough space
- child cyclists, in particular, have little road sense
- children often show off
- brakes can be faulty
- many do not have lights or wear helmets
- road safety teaching often poor
- too few cycle lanes.

**Statistics are frightening:**
- 9 out of 10 young cyclists know virtually nothing of the Highway Code
- over 60% of parents are happy to let children cycle without helmets
- 50% of motorists say they narrowly avoided a cyclist in the last month
- 89% of cyclists say they have nearly been knocked off in the last month.

**Remedies needed:**
- cycle paths
- better government transport policy
- driver and cyclist education
- consideration by road users
- speed reductions for cars.

**Task 2**

Design two layouts – one for each of the following:

- a leaflet for primary school children about road safety
- a magazine article aimed at parents on the same subject.

**Sketch** your layouts, considering the use of columns, boxes, etc.
Write **headings** in full; otherwise, show briefly what you would include, and where.

> Layout & Style/Language = Genre
> **REMEMBER!**

**Task 3**

For each layout, write *four* reasons why you included particular features.
Look at these examples for the primary leaflet.

> **Primary Leaflet**
> 1. I used the cartoon because …
> 2. The short paragraphs were supposed to …

**PRACTICE**

Unit 5  *Genres*  25

## PRACTICE

## Language styles

As you know, words and expressions must:
- be chosen with care
- suit the purpose and audience.

Read this news item:

> Yesterday, in Plymouth, Steven Varley, a 19-year-old electrician, won what was probably the strangest competition ever organised in Great Britain. He managed to swallow seventy-seven pickled gherkins in less than five minutes, despite hanging upside down from a sixty-foot high crane. He beat five other competitors, who only managed to eat sixty gherkins between them. A delighted Steven said he had been training for two months. However, he advised young children not to try to copy him. He does not wish to be responsible for young people falling out of bedroom windows.

### Task 4

*Headline writing*

Write a headline for this story which would be suitable for:

1. A tabloid newspaper
2. A broadsheet newspaper
3. A teenage magazine
4. *Pickles Express*: the trade magazine for grocery departments

### Task 5

Read the following extracts. In each case:

a) Write down what genre you think each comes from (probably).
b) List the words or phrases used which are typical of the particular genre.

1. Jones won the ball and, on the stroke of half time, volleyed it into the top corner. The stadium erupted.
2. My darling, each moment without you seems an hour.
3. Quite simply, politicians must act. As we hear regularly in parliament, the Third World is crippled with debt; but when are western democracies going to show common sense and compassion?
4. Do not think this is a problem you cannot overcome. You can be certain that he is suffering too. Together, you can come through it and your relationship will be stronger.
5. Our product is brighter, cleaner and tougher. It is the future.
6. A man was arrested yesterday for the theft of two hundred boxes of designer trainers in Derby last April.

### Task 6

For each of the extracts, write the next sentence, continuing in the same style.

# Extension Work: Letter writing

There is often a question which involves letter writing in Section B.

## Task 7

**Re-draft the following letter. There is no need to change the main ideas, but make it appropriate by changing the:**
- layout
- style.

Set it out as a **formal letter**, with an argument to persuade the Prime Minister.

> 17 Railway Cuttings,
> Stanwell,
> Chiselholme
> CH9 8RN
>
> 7 March
>
> Dear Tony,
> You look like a nice man and I am having trouble with the headteacher at my local school, so I'm writing to you for help. As my friend Eric said, "If the Prime Minister can't help you, what's the use of voting?" Eric's just been voted on to the local fishing club's fund raising committee, and I trust him. Anyway, that's why I'm writing to you.
>
> You see, the headmaster has just brought in a new rule about the colour of students' hair, and my daughter has had her hair dyed blue and he won't let her go back to lessons until she changes it and she says she won't. I don't think her education should be stopped just because she has got blue hair, do you?
>
> Can you have a word with him? His name's Moorby. He won't listen to me. You believe in fairness, and I think you might be able to do the trick.
>
> Let me know what you think.
> Cheers,
>
> Stella Brittan (Mrs)

**Examiner's Summary**
- Read widely, to develop knowledge of different genres.
- Analyse text, by considering intended purpose and audience.
- When writing, make layout and language appropriate for the question.

# Unit 6  A Writing Process for Section B

*Targets*

1. **To identify purpose and audience.**
2. **To plan by**
   - **structuring a response**
   - **using a 'language palette' to enrich your writing.**
3. **To write accurately.**
4. **To check properly.**

### FACTS
- Time
- Length

Section B of both Paper 1 and Paper 2 involves writing continuously, at some length. In each examination, you are allowed **an hour** to plan and produce a response of about **two sides** in length.

Those who write *much more* are likely to be less controlled and to make more errors. Those who write *much less* are unlikely to include enough detail to merit higher grades.

These responses produce half your examination marks in English – 30% of your final total – so it is essential that you have **a writing process**: a clear system which
- you can use every time and gives you confidence
- gives your writing a structure
- allows you to develop your ideas fluently.

### Skill 1: Identification of purpose and audience

It is essential that you identify the purpose and audience.

**FOCUS**
Purpose
Audience

| The purpose | The audience |
|---|---|
| This is the reason for writing; it is the *item* you have been asked to produce: a *letter about homelessness*, an *article about the dangers of fireworks*, etc. | This is the person/people for whom you are writing: *teenagers, old people,* etc. |

### Skill 2: Planning

You are advised to spend 10 minutes planning your response. Your plan must be detailed and organised, involving key ideas and essential vocabulary.

Invest 10 minutes every time: the better the plan, the better the writing.

### Skill 3: Writing

Follow your plan, otherwise time has been wasted and organisation will be poor.

### Skill 4: Checking

You should spend 5 to 10 minutes checking your work for errors and adding anything you have missed. Read your response in your head, but as if you were reading it out loud: it will be easier to spot poor expression, missing words and punctuation.

## How to follow the process

### Skill 1: Identification of purpose and audience

Underline or highlight the purpose and audience in the question.
This will help you stay 'on track' as you plan and write.

Read the following exam questions:

> **Question 1:**
> Write an article for an old people's magazine, persuading the readers to take care in the kitchen.
>
> **Question 2:**
> Write a set of instructions for primary school children, telling them about necessary safety rules for the home.

**Question 1:**

The audience

Write an article for an old people's magazine, persuading the reader to take care in the kitchen

The purpose and item

Unit 6   A Writing Process for Section B   29

**FOCUS: Planning**

### Task 1

Write down the purpose, item and audience for Question 2.

You will see immediately why careful planning is necessary.

With more areas of the home to deal with in Question 2, examination time would have to be used differently. Kitchen safety would take all of your time in the first response but just part of your time in the second.

In addition, you would use different language, depending on the ages of the readers.

### Task 2

a) Write a list of points to mention concerning safety in the kitchen.
b) Write a list of extra points you would add if writing about safety in the home.

### Skill 2: Planning

Here, we offer a planning system in five stages:

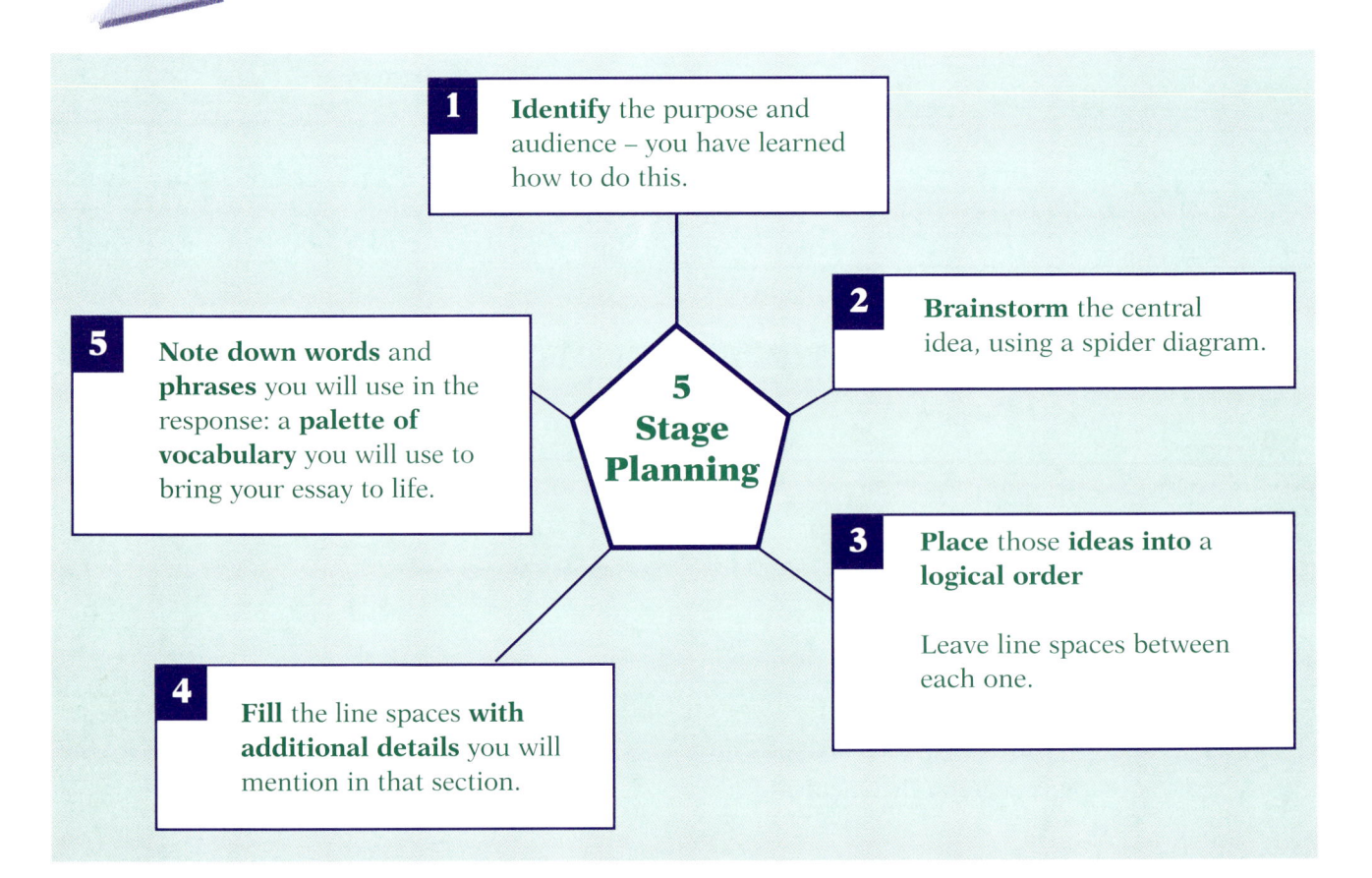

**5 Stage Planning**

1. **Identify** the purpose and audience – you have learned how to do this.

2. **Brainstorm** the central idea, using a spider diagram.

3. **Place** those **ideas into** a **logical order**

    Leave line spaces between each one.

4. **Fill** the line spaces **with additional details** you will mention in that section.

5. **Note down words** and **phrases** you will use in the response: a **palette of vocabulary** you will use to bring your essay to life.

Unit 6  A Writing Process for Section B

**Question:**
Write a letter to the government, to persuade politicians to give more money to improve IT facilities in schools.

**PRACTICE**

**Brainstorm**

*Spider diagram centred on "IT FACILITIES" with branches:*
- fewer exclusions
- better exam results
- teaching tailored more for individuals
- appeal to boys?
- students enjoy school more
- improved staff/student relations
- prepare students for the modern world
- Internet connections to other schools
- use of Internet by more students
- encourages private study/self-help
- more technological success in the future for Britain

**Plan and additional details**

**Introduction**
More money for IT will benefit students, schools, and the country

**1. Advantages for Students**

*Students will enjoy school more*
IT very popular. Computers in many homes already. Move away from the tedium of writing.

*Appeal to boys*
Boys love computers. Interest them in learning. Something they do well. Examples from my school. But don't leave out girls.

*Better exam results*
Response would be immediate. Boys, especially, would achieve more. Packages could be aimed precisely at individual needs.

*Would encourage private study/self-help ...*

**2 Advantages for Schools**

**Task 3**

Complete this plan, using the ideas from the spider diagram, and filling in the 'line spaces', as above, with extra details.

Unit 6 A Writing Process for Section B

**Vocabulary Palette**

Look at this palette of useful words and phrases.

Nevertheless

However

There are many examples in my own school

Money can be found for wars but perhaps education is less important?

Furthermore

Which countries are improving fastest?

Surely no one could disagree

We have to pledge ourselves to improvement

On the other hand

Contrary to popular opinion

### Task 4

Draw your own palette, and write down four potentially useful words and phrases, one from each of the following areas:

- **rhetorical** phrases intended to rouse our emotions ('surely no one could disagree ...')

- **ironical** phrases which use **sarcasm** or **humour** ('money can be found for wars but ...')

- any phrases you feel will be **effective** ('we must stride forward ...')

- **discourse markers** that link ideas (like 'however', 'nevertheless', etc.).

**The Invisible Palette**
**EXAMINER'S TIP!**

Of course, in the exam, you may not have time to draw a palette, but jot down key words and phrases, as if from an imaginary palette, ready to 'paint on to' your essay.

## Extension Work: The response itself – the IT letter

### Skill 3: Writing

Now you should be ready to write the letter. Of course, you will need to set it out properly; but you should find it relatively easy to produce, because most of the hard work has already been done.

However, there are skills to emphasise at this point:

1. **Spelling**
   - Many mistakes can be avoided: look particularly for doubling of letters, use of 'their', 'there', 'they're', etc.
2. **Expression**
   - Don't repeat yourself.
   - Use words and phrases that are appropriate for the intended audience.
3. **Punctuation**
   - Keep re-reading your response as you write it, and correct punctuation.
   - When you pause, consider using a full stop, comma or question mark.
   - If you can use commas, colons and semi-colons properly, show the examiner!
   - Don't forget apostrophes.
4. **Paragraphing**
   - One-sentence paragraphs or very long rambling ones usually suggest this is likely to be an 'E Grade' candidate.
   - Paragraphs that are all the same length usually indicate 'D Grade' work.
   - A variety of paragraph lengths suggest A*–C standard.
   - Paragraphs that contain flowing sentences and are linked well come from the best candidates.

### Task 5

**Write the first four or five paragraphs of your letter.**

Use your plan and keep re-reading the title.

### Skill 4: Checking

### Task 6

a) Re-read the advice above and correct your response.
b) Count how many improvements you have made!

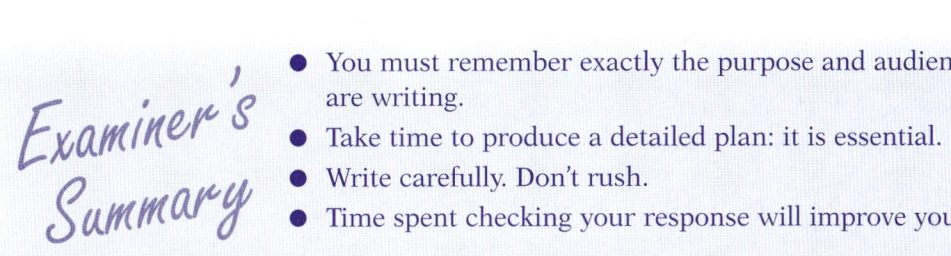

*Examiner's Summary*
- You must remember exactly the purpose and audience for which you are writing.
- Take time to produce a detailed plan: it is essential.
- Write carefully. Don't rush.
- Time spent checking your response will improve your mark.

# Unit 7  Revising Writing Skills

**Target**: To improve presentational, technical and compositional skills.

**Good technical skills = Good grades**

Section B of both English papers tests writing skills.
Assessment is made on the content of responses and on your ability to write:
- accurately
- neatly
- fluently.

This unit highlights technical skills needed for better grades.

**Spelling: what the levels mean**

| Grade | Statement | Meaning |
| --- | --- | --- |
| 'E Grade' | 'accurate basic spelling' | Common words spelt correctly |
| 'C Grade' | 'spelling generally accurate' | Most spellings correct |
| 'A Grade' | 'high level of technical ability' | Very few errors |

It is unlikely that you will suddenly improve all spellings overnight, but you can improve in key areas:

1. Ensure you can spell all the words used regularly on your palette.

2. Learn discourse markers, such as 'nevertheless', 'however', etc.

### Task 1

Ask a friend to dictate to you the opening paragraph from a text you have studied. Afterwards, mark it together to check for accuracy. If you made a mistake, are you able to identify why you did it (e.g. it sounded like another spelling)?

**Borrow Spellings! EXAMINER'S TIP!**

For Paper 1, you can **borrow** vocabulary from the texts in Section A – make sure you copy the words correctly.
Try checking your spellings from the last to the first, when you finish writing. This will help you to concentrate on the words, and not the flow of the text.

**Punctuation**

| Grade | Statement | Meaning |
|---|---|---|
| 'F Grade' | 'Generally accurate punctuation of sentences.' | This means using **full-stops** and **capital letters.** |

To gain higher marks, use: **commas** (to help make sense of your sentences).

### Task 2

Find a newspaper or magazine, and underline all the commas in three reports. Then read the sentences out loud, noticing how the commas are used. Finally, write three sentences in which you include commas.

| Colons | Semi-colons |
|---|---|
| ● follow a general statement, to introduce lists | ● break up complicated lists |
| ● or introduce quotations. | ● or separate closely-related sentences. |

Example: *I want to be like my father when I'm older: as intelligent as a chess Grand Master; as sophisticated as a member of the aristocracy; and as gentle as a hungry Rottweiler. Of course, he thinks he's nothing special; all fathers are modest. As he says to us at meal-times: "I am but a humble soul ..."*

### Task 3

Write three sentences, like the ones above, which include colons and semi-colons.

### Apostrophes

You will have covered these rules before, but as a quick reminder use:

**apostrophes of omission** – something has been left out, e.g. 'do not' becomes 'don't'; 'I am' becomes 'I'm'.
**apostrophes of possession** – something is owned, e.g. 'the room of the girl' becomes 'the girl's room'; 'the room of the girls' becomes 'the girls' room'.

**Apostrophe Rules REMINDER!**

### Speech marks

This passage (continued overleaf) will help you to remember the layout and form.

'I can do simple speech marks,' said Sadie.
Jamie replied, 'I can do them when the name of the person who's speaking comes first.'

**Layout and Form REMINDER!**

Unit 7 Revising Writing Skills

"It gets more difficult," said Steph, "when the speaker comes in the middle of the words spoken and is mentioned in the middle of a sentence."
"Sometimes it's slightly easier, though," said Sanjay. "Use a full stop if the speaker is mentioned when one sentence finishes and before the next one starts."
"But don't forget when to close speech marks. Only close them when the speaker finishes, no matter how many sentences she speaks," said Sarah.
"True! And there can only be one speaker in each paragraph," added the teacher.

### Task 4

Write ten lines of conversation about the current state of your GCSE work, using the same style of conversation as the one above. Include speech marks and at least four apostrophes.

| Question marks | Exclamation marks |
|---|---|
| You will know when and how to use question marks, but remember that it is easy to forget to use them in the stress of examinations. | Use exclamation marks sparingly, even when writing speech. Some candidates tend to use them to end every sentence. You should use them only to indicate: <br>• suddenness of expression <br>• surprise <br>• or to show something is remarkable. |

### Expression
'C Grade' candidates use words and phrases which are interesting enough to make the reader want to read more.

### Vocabulary
You must develop your vocabulary. New words need to be met 'in context' – in stories and articles you read. For English examinations, particularly Paper 1, you can find appropriate words in broadsheet newspapers.

### Task 5

a) Find **five** new words each day in the newspaper.
b) Use a dictionary to discover what they mean.
c) Learn them and put them into practice sentences.

### Originality
Avoid clichés (phrases we have all heard many times before). Instead, develop new vocabulary, similes or metaphors.

Rather than:
*'That soap opera is rubbish. It's like watching paint dry.'*
Consider:
*'That soap opera is as riveting as assemblies about litter.'*

Unit 7  *Revising* Writing Skills

Try to **'show'**, rather than **'tell'**.

Rather than:
*'I was bored and restless.'*
Consider:
*'I sat idly flicking through a creased magazine, or wandered up and down the corridor, checking the large cream clock on the dull wall ...'*

## Task 6

**Using the skills above, describe waiting for a train on an empty platform.**
- Include two similes and two metaphors of your own.
- Try not to tell the reader your feelings, but show them in actions or behaviour.

**Sentence construction**
Notice how a simple sentence can be developed:

1. I love you.
2. Despite your nose, I love you.
3. Despite your nose, which sports more spots than a Dalmatian, I love you.
4. Despite your nose, which sports more spots than a Dalmatian, I love you and everything about you.
5. Despite your nose, which sports more spots than a Dalmatian, I love you and everything about you, especially that big fat wallet packed with money you showed me on Saturday night ...

## Task 7

**Write a simple sentence about food, then build on to it, like in the example above. Start with: 'I love ...'.**

**Paragraphing: what the levels mean**

| Grade | Paragraph Types |
| --- | --- |
| 'E Grade' | Few paragraphs |
| 'D Grade' | Paragraphs are same length |
| 'C Grade' | Paragraph length varies appropriately to the meaning |
| 'B Grade' | Paragraphs begin to help move the writing forward |

Notice how stories and articles use paragraphs to make points simply, describe or build to a climax. Try to use paragraphs effectively in your own writing.

Write two sides, as advised on the examination paper. Writing more can lead to poor presentation.

If you find yourself designing a leaflet or magazine page, do sketching quickly: only handwriting is being assessed.

Presentation
**REMEMBER!**

# Unit 8 Writing to Argue

**Targets**
1. To learn how to construct an argument.
2. To consider different approaches to argumentative writing.
3. To examine beginnings and endings.
4. To follow the Writing Process.

**Skill 1: How to construct an argument**

To argue, you must be aware that there is an alternative viewpoint.
Do not just state what you believe; try to counter alternative points that
- have been made

or
- could be made.

An argument is effective if it convinces the reader or gives the reader cause to reconsider an opinion.

'Writing to Argue' requires:

- a strong beginning and ending
- a logical structure
- details which can be used as 'proof'
- an understanding of the alternative viewpoint
- logic which overcomes that other viewpoint.

**FOCUS: Argumentative Writing**

**Skill 2: Approaches to argumentative writing**

There are many possible approaches. Two, in particular, are worth consideration:

- A two-part response which states one case, then counters it with another.
- A piece written from one point of view but which makes reference to an alternative viewpoint, when appropriate.

## Skill 3: Beginnings and endings

The most basic organisation for an argumentative piece of writing is:

| • Opening: say what your point of view is. | • Middle: explain your points in detail. | • End: sum up by re-stating your main argument. |

However, it is important that

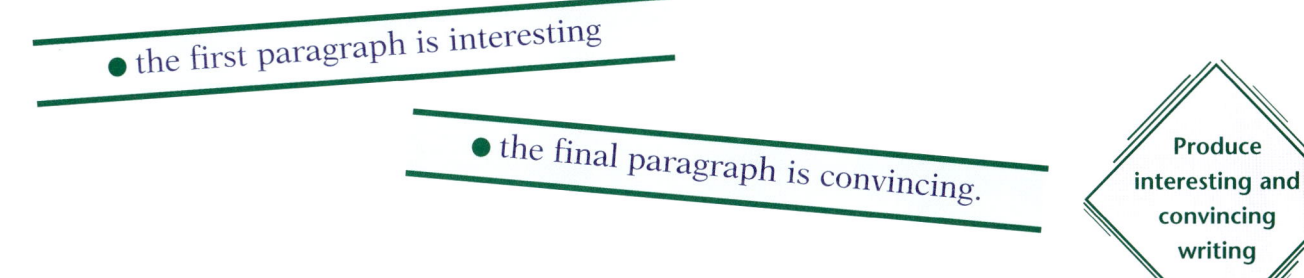

- the first paragraph is interesting
- the final paragraph is convincing.

**Produce interesting and convincing writing**

## Skill 4: The writing process

To be successful, you should follow the routine established in Unit 6 (page 30):

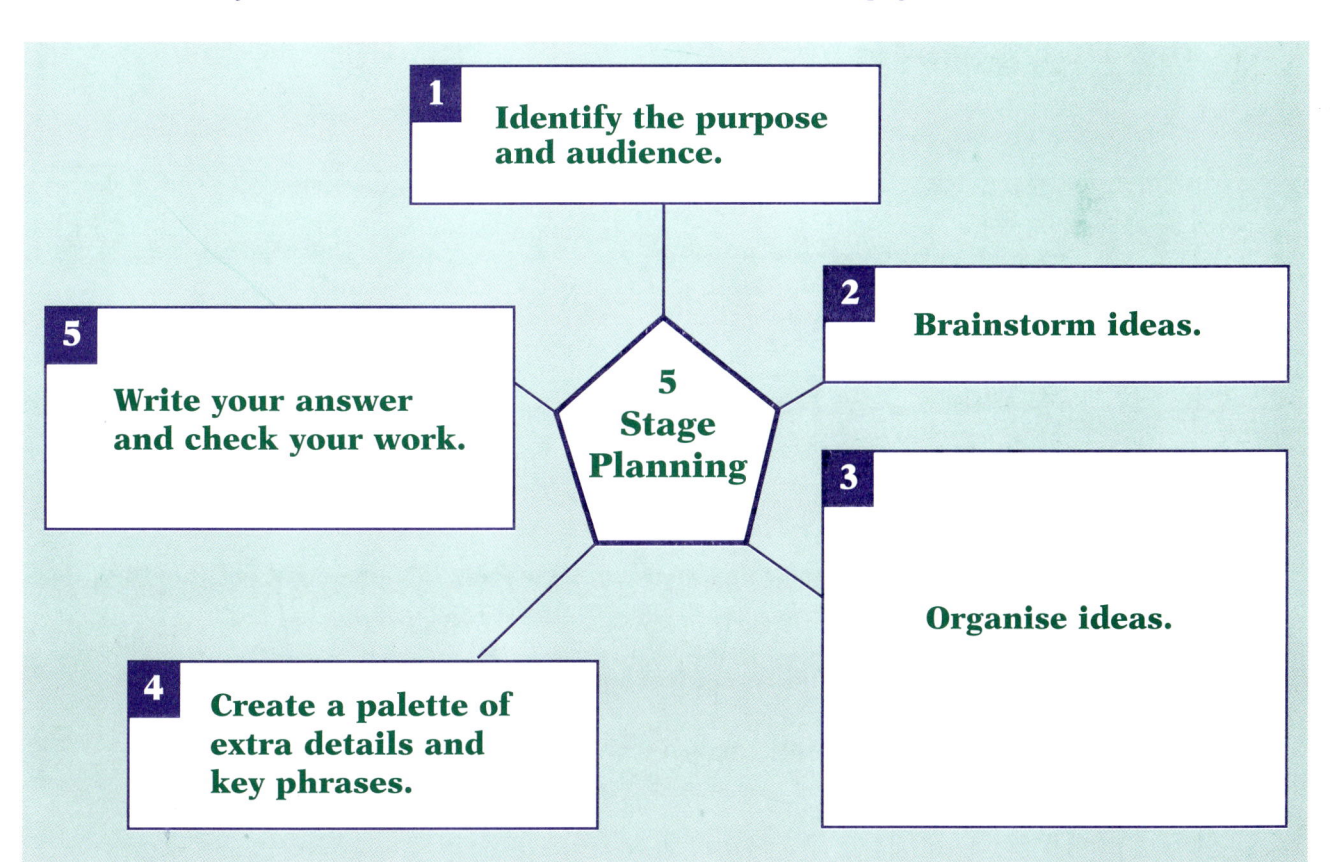

**5 Stage Planning**

1. Identify the purpose and audience.
2. Brainstorm ideas.
3. Organise ideas.
4. Create a palette of extra details and key phrases.
5. Write your answer and check your work.

Unit 8 Writing to Argue

39

## PRACTICE

Read this question:

Write a <u>speech</u> for a <u>conference about transport,</u> in which you <u>argue</u> that <u>no one should be charged to travel on buses.</u>

**Stages 1 and 2**

Brainstorm ideas and create a palette (we have done this for you).

### Brainstorm

**For charging**

otherwise money needed from tax-payers
unfair on those who need to use cars
buses unreliable: would be more so without proper funding

bus service would collapse
something for nothing never works

funding would be taken from health and education?

**Against charging**

more would use buses
safer roads
more buses so more jobs
fewer cars so less pollution
traffic jams fewer
better bus services would result
more sociable to travel elsewhere with others
better transport policy for new century

### Task 1

**FOCUS: Using Logic**

**You decide to answer this question by writing the argument for charging, then putting more strongly the argument against charging.**

Write down the points above in a logical order – the order you would choose.

(For this exercise, only concern yourself with organising the above ideas.)

Unit 8  Writing to Argue

Now look at this palette of key phrases and words.

## Palette

*however*
*nevertheless*
*in contrast*
*on the other hand*

*more consideration for the environment*
*over-reliance on the motor car*
*health must come before convenience*

### Task 2

Copy out this palette and add to it.

**FOCUS: Using a Palette**

**Stage 3: Writing**

Read this example of a possible opening to the essay:

*It is clear that, as a society, we must change our attitude to travel. The car has had its day; environmental considerations are now more important. It is vital that more people begin to use the buses again so that …*

### Task 3

Complete the paragraph, then write the first sentence of the next one, covering the first point you placed in your plan.

Now read this ending, which is equally firm:

*Politicians are intelligent. In time, they will come to accept that free buses will benefit us all, getting cars off the roads. People will be happy to use them …*

### Task 4

Add *three* more sentences to this ending, to *sum up* your argument and convince your audience that no one should be charged to travel on a bus.

**Interesting & Convincing Writing = Marks**
**REMEMBER!**

Unit 8 Writing to Argue — 41

## PRACTICE

## Rhetoric, second-guessing and anecdotes

If you concentrate on one point of view, and do not include a detailed alternative viewpoint, it allows more:
- time to put your own argument
- space in which to develop your points.

Here are three techniques you can use:

### 1 Rhetorical questions

These raise the emotions of the reader and do not expect an answer.

Example: *We all know that things need to change, don't we? We have been told about what is happening to the environment; how long will it be before we start to do something about it?*

### Task 5

Write one or two sentences in which you use rhetorical questions to support your argument for free buses.

### 2 Second-guessing

When you predict in advance what the objections might be and answer them.

Example: *Although some might say that giving more public funding to buses will mean less money for the health service, this does not have to be the case …*

As you can see, even though you have mentioned the opposite argument, you can make it seem incorrect.

### Task 6

Write a sentence in which you mention the argument for paying bus fares, but make the argument seem incorrect. Start with 'Although' or 'In spite of' or 'Even though'.

### 3 Anecdotes

Short personal stories or accounts, which, in the case of argumentative writing, could prove your points.

Example: *My grandad could not afford the bus into town and did all his shopping locally. He had to pay more for his food than he would have done at a supermarket. He was poor and even though he had worked hard all his life he had to do without things. Free buses would make such a difference to old people and to poor people in general.*

Finally, a touch of humour, when appropriate, can enliven your writing:

> *Of course, my grandad never trusted anybody. He wouldn't have boarded a free bus, in case it didn't have any brakes. He'd have made grandma try it out first ...*

### Task 7

Write any paragraph of your response. In it, use both anecdote and humour.

## Extension Work: The final response

These are the opening sentences for each paragraph of one response. Notice how the ideas seem to follow logically:

**Paragraph 1**
*Bus travel should be free ...*

**Paragraph 2**
*Those in charge of transport policy must realise that free buses would become full buses, because people would abandon cars to save money ...*

**Paragraph 3**
*Consequently, jobs would be created: bus drivers would be needed, and ...*

**Paragraph 4**
*Such a growth in public transport inevitably leads to improved services ...*

**Paragraph 5**
*What is more, travellers would become more sociable; they would no longer be sitting alone in their cars.*

**Paragraph 6**
*'Fewer motorists' means 'less pollution'.*

**Paragraph 7**
*Not only the air would improve, because there would be fewer traffic jams, but also the roads would be safer for pedestrians.*

**Paragraph 8**
*Surely, no one can argue convincingly against obvious improvements?*

### Task 8

Choose any three consecutive paragraphs and complete them, keeping the opening sentences as they are. Use the skills you have learnt.

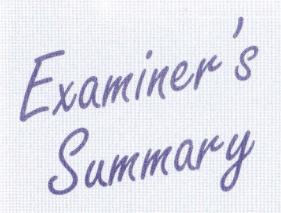

**Examiner's Summary**
- Argue against another viewpoint.
- Use rhetoric, anecdote, humour and 'second-guessing', when appropriate.
- Give special consideration to introductions and conclusions.

# Unit 9  Writing to Persuade

**Targets**
1. To construct a persuasive argument.
2. To use rhetorical and emotive techniques, anecdote and humour.
3. To write an effective opening and ending.

**FOCUS: Using Persuasive Language**

Some tasks in the exam require you to 'persuade' or use 'persuasion'. This might seem the same as being asked to 'argue' a point. However, there are subtle differences. Generally speaking when you seek to 'persuade' you:

- don't simply state the case for or against a point of view
- tend to be more subjective, more personal, and more one-sided
- try to get a more emotional response from your readers.

However, you do often use similar techniques as those covered in Unit 8, 'Writing to Argue', such as using rhetoric, anecdotes and so on (page 42).

The sorts of questions you might be asked in the exam are as follows.

### 'Formal' Questions

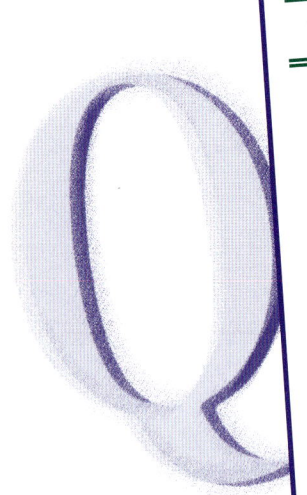

These are quite close in style and content to an 'argue'-style question, the only difference being, perhaps, that you do not put the other case.

Examples:

'Write a letter to your local council to persuade it to improve health services in your area.'

'Write an article for a national newspaper, to persuade the readers to campaign for closer links with Europe.'

'Write a leaflet to persuade the public to oppose the factory farming of animals.'

## Less Formal Questions

These sorts of questions are quite different, and expect a persuasive response to a less contentious (perhaps less serious) subject – one about which few would argue.

Examples:

'Write a speech for your year group, persuading them to help you raise money for a new youth centre.'

'Write an article for a teenage magazine. Persuade the readers your favourite group or singer is the best in the business.'

'Write a leaflet to persuade children not to begin smoking.'

Learn persuasive techniques by noticing how those around you persuade others. For example, count the number of different techniques used by a teacher in any lesson; and how parents deal with young children.

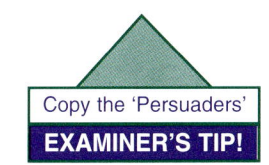

**EXAMINER'S TIP!** Copy the 'Persuaders'

Question: You have been corresponding on the Internet with a boy or girl from another country. He or she has asked you to write in person to them. Write a <u>letter</u> to <u>persuade</u> your <u>foreign pen friend</u> to <u>visit</u> you for <u>the summer.</u>

**PRACTICE**

**Brainstorm**

*help learn even better English*

*chance to see the country*

*break from own family*

**Visit**

**Task 1**

**Complete the spider diagram.**

Unit 9 Writing to Persuade

**Task 2**

Organise the ideas into a logical order: the order in which you would write about them.

**Remember!**

> Ideas should be clustered into sections, so that they have something in common, and follow sensibly from what you have just been saying.

**Focus: Planning**

**Persuasive Language**

Normally, you would now create a palette of extra ideas, words and phrases to use. First, let's look at the language used in persuasive responses.

Read these paragraphs:

1. When here, you will visit many places like Wales, Devon, the Lake District, Stratford upon Avon, Edinburgh, York and London. I'll take you to castles like Caernarvon, Leeds and Warwick. You'll have an opportunity to see other countries without paying a penny.

2. Will you ever again have a chance to see so many places that are highlighted in the guidebooks? You can visit Wales, with its own people and traditions; Devon, full of rolling hills and cream teas; the Lake District, once the home of the Romantic Poets; Shakespeare's birthplace in Stratford upon Avon; and famous cities such as York, Edinburgh and London. The castles will amaze you: Caernarvon, Leeds, Warwick and many more, equally stunning. You won't have to pay a penny for all this: can you afford to turn down such an offer?

**Task 3**

Note down any differences between Paragraphs 1 and 2. Think about the use of emotive and rhetorical language and visual imagery.

**Task 4**

Now write the palette for your letter – that is, your own selection of key emotive and rhetorical phrases and, where relevant, visual imagery.

There are two other key elements which will help improve your grade.

**PRACTICE**

## 1. The Opening

Naturally, you want to interest the reader, so the use of **anecdote** – a brief story used to prove a point – can be used. It is useful at any stage; but is particularly effective at the start of a persuasive response.

Example

> Dear Lotte,
>
> I am still waiting to hear whether you can come to spend the summer with us. If you can't make up your mind, perhaps the story of what happened to my sister might persuade you.
>
> She was invited to spend two weeks with a family in America when she was sixteen and she had the time of her life. Apart from the fact that she learnt all about what Americans are really like, she also discovered that boys over there love an English accent. She was very popular and had more dates than my grandma eats at Christmas! (I hope you understand English jokes!) …

### Task 5

Now write a persuasive anecdote to go at the start of your letter. Add a touch of humour if you can, and if it is appropriate.

## 2. The Ending

Here are two possible types:
1. sum up what you have already said
or
2. produce a final, compelling touch of persuasion.

**Type 1**: summing up

> I hope I've managed to convince you to come and that you will write soon to say when you'll be arriving. Don't forget: a complete break, sightseeing and new friendships await you. Also, as I said, your English will improve, and you will be more likely to get that job working in a hotel abroad when you are older.
> It will be a wonderful holiday. Please come!

### Task 6

Write an ending to sum up the points in your letter.

Unit 9 Writing to Persuade

**Type 2**: compelling ending

*If I haven't yet managed to persuade you to come, you must bear in mind one last point. The biggest music festival Britain has ever seen will be taking place near here in August. Every top act will be appearing: you name them, they'll be there. Don't miss this opportunity! If you come, you'll be the envy of all your friends — and I mean all!*

### Task 7

Write an ending for your letter that includes a final, powerful point.

**Go For Better Grades!**

### Extension Work: Improved persuasion

Read this extract - it is 'A Grade' standard. The question asked students to compose a leaflet persuading people to contribute to a charity, called FamAid.

---

*Please support our fundraising for FamAid. Across the world, young children are starving and need help from organisations like ours, if they are to survive.*

*On a recent trip to India, I held a tragic young baby who died only minutes later. It is not something a person could ever forget. Can you pretend deaths like this are not happening? Or should we all be involved in creating a more humane world?*

*I believe there is nothing more pitiful than a child's cry but children are crying in half the countries in the world. They cry to us and we must care.*

---

### Task 8

a) Note down the three most effective phrases or sentences.
b) Say whether they are emotive, rhetorical or anecdotal and why they are effective.

Unit 9  Writing to Persuade

> **Task 9**
>
> Read this 'D' standard extract.

> We need a new common room for Year 11 and are raising as much money as we can. You are the Headteacher and I hope you will help us. You could ask parents to give us support. You could ask the school governors as well. I am sure you can see we deserve some help and we are confident you have the influence to get us what we need.

Re-write the extract, developing the sentences and the extract as a whole.

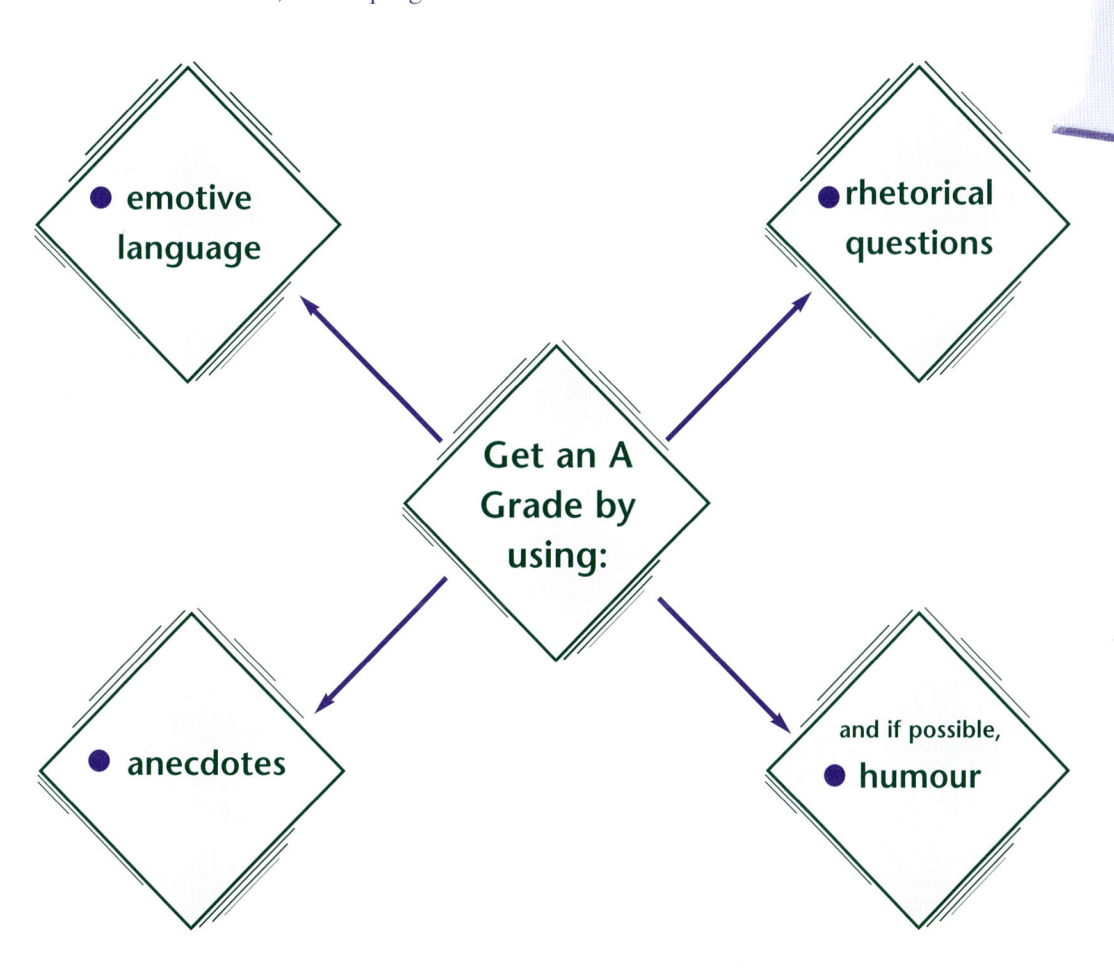

**Get an A Grade by using:**

- emotive language
- rhetorical questions
- anecdotes
- and if possible, humour

### Examiner's Summary

Follow the Writing Process you have now learned.

- Use rhetorical questions, emotive language, anecdote, imagery.
- Use humour, where appropriate.
- Make the opening and ending effective.
- Learn the art of persuasion from those around you.

Unit 9 Writing to Persuade

# Unit 10 Writing to Instruct

**Targets**

1. To organise instructions effectively.
2. To identify the tone for instructions.
3. To identify different forms of instructional writing.
4. To understand what is required for top grades.
5. To fulfil the Writing Process.

Instructional writing involves very precise **expression** and **organisation of ideas**: this is the crucial element.

### Planning your response

The Writing Process should be followed, as usual. However, when planning, the instructions must be in logical stages, otherwise:

**FOCUS: The Writing Process**

- they make no sense

or

- they seem random and lose their impact.

So, if you were asked for instructions on organising a charity rounders match, you might:

1. say why this is an appropriate way of raising money.

Then write about how to:

2. sort out the venue
3. arrange publicity
4. organise the competition
5. deal with spectators
6. successfully finish with presentations
7. clear away afterwards
8. deal with the money collected.

### Technique

- If bullet points are provided in the question, make them your basic planning framework.

- Then use sub-headings, indicating different sections, beneath each bullet.

- Then plan more detailed points under each sub-heading.

**PRACTICE**

**Read the following question.**

Write instructions to be given to any new student joining your school.

Include instructions about:

- uniform
- behaviour
- homework
- lunchtime arrangements
- other rules
- how to survive in school!

### Task 1

**Jot down the purpose and audience, then brainstorm ideas to form the plan.**

Next, complete a plan: the first part has been started for you.

> Opening
>
> Uniform
> Boys: black blazer, silver and black tie, grey trousers, etc.
> Girls (you continue)
> Coats
> Games kit, etc.
>
> Behaviour...

### Task 2

**Have you completed your plan? If so, now complete your palette with discourse markers, and phrases with an imperative tone, which tell the reader what to do.**

For example:

| Above all, ensure ... | Make sure ... |
| Your first priority must be to ... | Avoid ... |

↑ discourse markers  ↑ imperative tone

Unit 10 Writing to Instruct

**When you finally begin writing, you must:**
- introduce your topic effectively
- adopt an appropriate tone
- make it clear that you know your audience
- identify the purpose of the instructions.

1. Your opening might be **impersonal** writing, dealing factually with a topic:

> **A** **B** **C**
> Thousands of people die on the roads each year. It is essential, therefore, that parents teach children all they need to know about road safety. This set of instructions will tell you clearly what to say and when to say it. **D**

2. Sometimes, it can be **less formal**:

> **A + B** **C + D**
> Since I know you are new to babysitting, I thought I'd better let you know all that I've learnt over the past two years. Believe me, it can be a rough ride looking after some of the little horrors; you can have nightmares for weeks. However, if you pay close attention to what I have to say, you should survive!

### Task 3

Write two openings for your instructions to new school students using:

a) a formal tone

b) a more friendly one.

Either would be appropriate in this instance.

After your opening, decide how to set out your instructions.

Consider these three techniques:

**A** Sub-headings, followed by
- numbered points, e.g. (1), (2), etc.

or
- bullet points.

**B** Sub-headings, introducing short paragraphs.

**C** Conventional essay form.

**PRACTICE**

Instructional writing is all around us.

For example, there should be fire evacuation instructions in your classroom. Read as much instructional writing as you can. Consider how it is:
- set out
- expressed.

**Look and Learn — EXAMINER'S TIP!**

*Example of instructions:* **Type A**

### SWIMMING POOL

**On arrival at the outdoor pool**

- apply suntan cream
- check the depth markers
- read any safety instructions
- notice where lifeguards and lifebelts are positioned.

**Task 4**

Use the same sub-heading, but change the swimming pool list from bullet points into a paragraph with connected sentences (Type B).

Try to vary your expression and avoid making it read like a list.

Unit 10 Writing to Instruct

Do not write:

> When you get there, apply suntan cream, check the depth markers ...

Instead, write something like:

> When you arrive at the pool, your first priority must be the safety of yourself and those with you. On sunny days, it is essential that you all apply suntan cream, to avoid the damaging effects of sunburn ...

**Go For Better Grades!**

## Extension Work: Developing instructions

The simplest instructions are just a list of points.

That can be appropriate, but GCSE examiners look for a wider range of skills.

No matter how good the ideas in your response, it is impossible to achieve top grades without using:

- discourse markers ('although', 'as a result of', etc.)
- a variety of sentence constructions
- a wide range of vocabulary
- devices like humour, anecdote and rhetoric.

For top grades, it becomes almost essential to adopt a conventional essay style, writing continuously and in paragraphs.

Read this extract from a 'C Grade' example:

*How to enjoy the evenings*

- *check the entertainments available*
- *decide which to try before you go out*
- *dress appropriately*
- *since it's a big resort, make sure you can find your way home later.*

Unit 10 Writing to Instruct

> *How to cope with an enraged landlady*
>
> *Landladies do not like you to arrive back at your lodgings after midnight, so:*
> - *always be polite*
> - *do not argue with her*
> - *once inside, go straight to bed*
> - *avoid her in the morning.*

Now read this extract from an 'A Grade' example. Look at the annotation showing how the candidate uses the appropriate skills.

> **Discourse markers**            **Rhetoric**
>
> Of course, we all go on holiday to enjoy the evenings, don't we? That's what being young is all about. However, to get the most out of what's available, it's best to follow certain guidelines. For example, find out what the resort has to offer. It's no good going out in just a t-shirt if you end up in an ice-skating arena, like I did once in Wales!
>
> **Anecdote and humour**      **Wide range of vocabulary**     **Variety of sentence constructions**
>
> So, check the local papers, ask around, then make a decision about what you intend to do for the next few hours. Dress accordingly – and conservatively, if necessary ...

## Task 5

Complete the 'A Grade' example, covering the points made by the 'C Grade' candidate.

Make sure you continue to include:
- discourse markers
- humour
- and rhetoric.

**Examiner's Summary**
- Fulfil the Writing Process.
- Pay attention to the organisation of ideas.
- Adopt an instructional tone.
- For top grades, develop beyond just the listing of ideas.

Unit 10 Writing to Instruct

# Unit 11 Writing to Inform

**Targets**
1. To identify purpose and audience.
2. To plan effectively.
3. To produce an informative response.
4. To develop the response logically and fluently.
5. To fulfil the Writing Process.

**Stage 1: Underlining or highlighting**
Underlining or highlighting reminds you what is required.
Slight differences in questions make a considerable difference to the response. What differences would result from the following titles?

1. Write a letter to a *close but ageing* relative to inform them about **how *you intend* to spend the summer holidays** following your GCSE exams.

2. Write a letter to a *close* relative to inform them **how, ideally, you *would like* to spend the summer holidays** following your GCSE exams.

**Stage 2: Structure**
Structure is always important. Plan to relay information logically and progressively:

- the opening paragraph should introduce the topic
- following paragraphs should provide development, using discourse markers like: *next, then, subsequently, afterwards, therefore,* etc.
- the response should draw to a definite conclusion.

**Stage 3: Relevance**
Check that your information is relevant to the title.

For example, if you are informing younger students about the demands of GCSE examinations, do not include your opinions of examination systems.

**Stage 4: Planning**
Planning is essential, to ensure you have not omitted something you later realise is important.

We say: "Oh, I forgot to mention earlier that…", but here you are writing. Details must not be forgotten. Impress the examiner with the fluency and organisation of your ideas.

*Impress the examiner with the fluency and organisation of your ideas*

## Stage 5: Follow your plan
The writing must follow your plan, to make the flow of your information convincing.

**PRACTICE**

Read this question:

Write a letter to inform <u>the person who employs you part-time</u> that you <u>have won a travel competition and will be unable to do your job for four weeks.</u>

### Task 1
**Brainstorm ideas.**

*apologies, excited, four weeks away, Win!, keep job open, part-time*

### Task 2
**Organise your ideas.**
Use the following sub-headings as your plan (they are relevant and could be joined together for a logical and fluent response):

- details about your win and how it will affect your job
- reasons why you wish to accept the voyage you have won
- why you hope the job will be kept open for you
- your feelings about your employer and/or employment
- a conclusion which sums up your feelings about the win and the job.

**Plan Using Sub-headings**

### Task 3
**Create your language palette.**

### Task 4
Next, consider the tone of your letter. Re-read the question, then decide which of these openings is most appropriate, and why:

**Example 1**
I have just won a competition and I am going abroad for a month and you will have to keep my job open for me.

**Example 2**
I am really excited. I entered a competition with a first prize of a cruise across to Africa: and I have won! Unfortunately, if I go away for four weeks, I will need an extended period of leave from my job. I am hoping that you will realise my trip is an opportunity I can't refuse, and that you might be prepared to keep my job open for me until I return …

### Task 5

**Write your own opening.**
Make sure it:
- reminds your employer of what, exactly, your job involves
- gives details of the competition
- says when you need to be away
- asks for permission to take an extended holiday.

**PRACTICE**

You are going to link your opening to the next section of your plan.

### Task 6

Write two sentences, either of which could be used to begin your next paragraph, which will give reasons why you wish to accept the voyage you have won.

Begin your sentences with the following discourse markers:
- *Of course,*
- *As you will appreciate,*

### Task 7

Choose the best opening sentence, and then write the remainder of the section (this can be one paragraph, or more).

### Task 8

Now write the section in which you say why you hope the job will be kept open for you. You will need a sentence which moves you on from what has gone before: for example, '*I understand, however, that all holidays must come to an end*', **or something similar. Try to create a link of your own.**

Following your linking sentence, you must **inform** your employer exactly
- why you need/want the job
- or how you can help him or her in the long run, if you can keep the job.

**Extra Development**
**EXAMINER'S TIP!**

Do not feel that each point in any plan must be covered in a single paragraph. Sometimes further, vital, development will be needed, which will require extra paragraphs.

### Task 9

Complete your response, using appropriate linking sentences.
Your tone should still be positive but apologetic.

## Extension Work: Improving the grade

Here, we look at how to improve a 'D Grade' piece of writing.

The following extracts are from students who were asked to write a speech, to inform a group of headteachers what pupils think about the education system. The first is from a 'D Grade' response.

> I have just told you about some school rules that students hate, and now I want to tell you about what we think about school uniform. Some people like it but most people don't like it. It is old fashioned. We don't want to wear ties, because they stifle us. In summer we are much too hot. Also, the colours are terrible. We want to wear things that are cool. We want to wear trainers too.

### Task 10

Re-write the extract, using:
- less repetition (e.g. 'we want')
- better links between sentences
- rhetorical questions and humour.

Below is an 'A Grade' paragraph.

> There are numerous other points about which we might complain. For example, why do we have to start school at nine o'clock? Is it just because our parents want us out of the house so they can go to work? A poll of school students would show clearly that the majority would prefer a system of flexi-time, so that they could work at the time of day which suits them best. Teachers refuse to accept that it is almost impossible to be enthusiastic about French verbs before your breakfast has even reached your stomach; but students know the truth. They know that if the government is serious about raising standards of education, it should allow students to stay in bed until they feel able to cope with school's demands.

### Task 11

**Identify the ways in which the 'A grade' candidate followed the advice in Task 10.**

*Examiner's Summary*

- Always plan carefully.
- Ensure your response is informative and that you are answering the question.
- Link ideas effectively.
- Make sure you move smoothly from an introduction to a logical conclusion.
- Fulfil the Writing Process.

# Unit 12 Writing to Explain

**Targets**
1. To identify purpose and audience.
2. To plan the response.
3. To ensure the content is appropriate and engaging.

**1** **Purpose and Audience**
When writing to explain, you will usually concentrate on the **purpose**. You might have to explain how:
- something works or is organised.

But you will probably write about how:
- something or someone has affected you.

So, the **audience** will be the examiner. You can write more personally.

**Exemplar Question:**
Explain how an incident in your school career has affected your attitude to education.

**2** **Planning**
Brainstorm, then organise your ideas.

**Know Yourself**
**EXAMINER'S TIP!**

As a general rule, write about what you know about. If it's something you have simply seen on television, you are unlikely to be convincing.

In this case, your response needs:
- an introduction, showing you are dealing with the title
- a series of connected paragraphs, explaining what happened to you
- a conclusion, which explains how you have been affected.

You would also need the usual language palette:
- discourse markers
- and an assortment of other words and phrases.

**3** **Being appropriate and engaging**
Do exactly what you have been asked to do. For example, for the question above, you would **not** write about a friend's experience. Getting the purpose wrong severely affects your mark.

In this case, to make the writing **engaging** (to hold the examiner's attention) you should make the reader:

Unit 12 Writing to Explain

- feel the incident really happened
- understand exactly what it was like to be there
- believe such an incident must have changed your life.

Emotion and precise details are essential.

**Emotion and precise details are essential**

**PRACTICE**

**Read this question:**
Who is the <u>most interesting person</u> you have ever known? Explain <u>what the person is like or was like</u> and the <u>effect they have had on other people.</u>

The **audience** is the examiner. Notice:
- the **purpose** is to write about someone who is **interesting**
- and you must explain the effect they have on **others**, not just yourself.

This, therefore, is a strange mixture:
- why *you* think they are interesting
- how *others* are affected.

### Task 1

**Brainstorm and organise the response.**

| Use these sub-headings to organise your ideas: | ● the person ● why they are interesting ● their effect on others ● the ending: what, exactly, is interesting about the person. |

Always try to think of material which is unlikely to be produced by anyone else. It might be an eccentric member of your family; a person from your childhood in another area; or someone who featured in a strange, or memorable event.

**Be Original**
**EXAMINER'S TIP!**

If you have followed the above bullet points, your response will be **appropriate**.

To make it **engaging**, you might include:
- physical description
- the person's psychological impact on people
- anecdote
- conversation, to help the person 'come to life'
- similes and metaphors
- humour.

### Task 2

**Write your language palette. Include phrases and details from the bullet points above.**

**PRACTICE**

Consider one candidate's opening:

> *I know a very interesting person. I see her every day. She is funny looking and even scares my dog, Snowy. Snowy isn't frightened of anyone else in the world.*

### Task 3

a) Write a list of what this candidate is doing right.
b) Re-write the opening, improving it by using:
- **longer, more complex sentences**
- **precise description of the person.**

Now, read another candidate's effort:

> *The first time I saw him, he was talking to a neighbour of ours, who has been in prison. However, the stranger was not frightening at all. He reminded me of one of those weathermen you see on the BBC. I guessed he was probably wearing a cardigan under his overcoat.*

### Task 4

Write notes to the following questions:
a) How are the sentences constructed and varied?
b) How is the reader supposed to react to the content? For example, did anything make you smile?
c) How is the writer beginning to show this person is interesting?
d) Which is better, the first or second extract?

### Task 5

Write your own opening. Bring your character to life, remembering to explain why he or she is interesting.

**Consider using ...**
- anecdotes
- simile or metaphor
- speech/dialogue
- a paragraph on each person who has been affected

### Task 6

Write the main, central, section of your response, i.e. why the person is interesting and how the person affects other people.

### Task 7

Write your ending. Include a summary of your feelings and the person's general effect on others. Begin with:
- *I always found her amazing, and so did everyone else.* Or
- *He terrified all of us, every member of the class.* Or
- Something similar, to link with what has gone before.

Unit 12 Writing to Explain

# Extension Work: A* quality

Read this 'A* Grade' extract:

> What is more, it was not just me who found her behaviour peculiar. Let's face it, any woman who rushes out into the street dressed only in a Union Jack and buys an ice cream for all the children is hardly likely to be considered normal; and when she danced out and started singing hymns to the church congregation as they left one Sunday, you would have had to be there to appreciate how funny it was. The vicar was speechless. Several very well-dressed ladies simply turned round and went back into the church. Most tried to just pretend she didn't exist.
>
> However, you could never ignore Mrs Decanniere. If there was a chance to be with people, she never missed it. She was gregarious as well as completely mad.
>
> I used to feel sorry for her husband as he persuaded her back into the darkness of their little house. He could have left her in an institution, but wanted her at home with him. He must have loved her, despite everything, but she seemed to be wearing him away as the years went by. He went greyer and his eyes became tired, almost desperate in a way. And at night, through the wall, we could sometimes hear him crying with her. Those who mocked her never knew how much sadness there was in that house …

## Task 8

Answer the following questions:
a) What do we learn about the writer's attitude to Mrs Decanniere?
b) How many people's reactions to her are included here, and how do they differ?
c) What is the effect of the short paragraph?
d) How does the writer make the woman and where she lives come to life?

Look back at your own response:
- Is it as lively as this one?
- Have you used anecdotes as successfully?
- Have you used a short paragraph for effect?
- Have you explained as clearly as this why the person is interesting?

*FOCUS: Sharpening Skills*

## Task 9

Re-write a section of your own response, incorporating the skills you have just been examining. Try to make it as good as the extract above.

**Examiner's Summary**
- Make sure you are doing exactly what the title demands.
- Write about things you have actually experienced.
- Make your writing lively.
- Conclude by summarising your thoughts about the topic.

# Unit 13 Writing to Describe

**Targets**
1. To describe exactly what is specified in the question.
2. To plan carefully.
3. To produce an interesting opening and an appropriate ending.
4. To make the description come to life.
5. To fulfil the Writing Process.

In descriptive writing, three elements are crucial:
- the opening
- the ending
- originality and vividness.

### The Opening

Imagine the examiner has been marking scripts for four or five hours each day for three weeks. It is midnight when he or she gets to your paper. You must grab the examiner's attention.

An effective opening paragraph puts you on your way to success.

### The Ending

In a description, instead of a formal conclusion, you could end:
- on a dramatic moment
- with a particular revelation
- with someone walking or driving away, into a new or better life
- or ...?

Whatever you choose, your ending should arise from what has gone before. It must be effective because after reading it the examiner awards your mark. It's your final chance to impress.

### Originality and Vividness

You can employ:
- your five senses to make a description sharper
- conversation to bring people and situations to life
- similes, metaphors, onomatopoeia and varied vocabulary to add interest.
- variety of sentence and paragraph length for effect.

Read this question:
Describe a <u>town or a village or part of a city</u> that <u>you know well.</u>

**PRACTICE**

### Task 1

**Decide what you intend to describe.**
Notice:
- You are not asked to write about the countryside, the beach, or a school. Or about somewhere you've never visited but that you have seen on television.
- It *must* be a town, village or part of a city you know well.

### Task 2

**Brainstorm your ideas.**
Include details like:

- the people
- buildings/areas of interest
- shops, restaurants and pubs
- traffic and road conditions
- the effect of the seasons
- war memorial

**Town**

Now organise your sub-headings from the diagram into a suitable order.

As you put the ideas into a sensible order, jot down, as part of your palette, the discourse markers you are likely to use to link your sections.

**EXAMINER'S TIP!** Jot down the discourse markers

### Task 3

**Produce the rest of your language palette, e.g. good phrases, extra details.**

### Task 4

**The opening: write four short openings to see which works best:**

| **A** Conversation: | **B** Description of the most important feature: | **C** Atmosphere: at a particular time of year or time of day: | **D** Description of a person: |
|---|---|---|---|
| a typical conversation between residents or visitors<br>or<br>an argument about the place<br>or<br>a conversation which mentions matters you will discuss later<br>or<br>any other conversation you think is appropriate. | a building<br>or<br>a square<br>or<br>a road<br>or<br>whatever. | describe what is happening and try to capture the place's mood. | choose a person who is at home in the environment and is naturally part of it. |

# PRACTICE

### Task 5

**Re-write *two* of your openings, adding any appropriate features you have left out from the list below:**
- use of senses: sight, touch, taste, hearing or smell
- conversation
- simile
- metaphor
- onomatopoeia
- variation of vocabulary (perhaps using local dialect in conversation)
- sentence length for effect.

In the exam you won't have time to re-write; the skills you learn now need to come automatically on the day.

**Re-draft Skills Now**
**EXAMINER'S TIP!**

### Task 6

**Select the better opening.**

### Task 7

**Write the central sections of your response.**
Keep the above list in mind and do not forget you are trying to impress a tired examiner! As you transform your plan into essay form, vary your paragraph length. Try using:

- **short paragraphs**
  to make actions seem more dramatic, or to highlight a specific idea or change of pace.

- **longer paragraphs**
  to convey a slower, more reflective mood, or when you are describing things in more detail. Also useful as a build-up of connected ideas, or short phrases, for example in a chase.

### Task 8

**Write your ending.**
Your final paragraph should grow naturally from what has gone before.
You might, for example, end with:
- a quotation about the place and, perhaps, some comment on it
- your personal feelings about the place
- an image that captures what you have put across in your response
- or a statement about why people stay/leave or why visitors return/don't return.

## Extension Work: Improving further

The following response received a top grade.

> *The town is vibrant. It hums with a music all its own. Babies cry, like they do anywhere; and men with red faces fall out of the bars into grey Saturday afternoons and laugh too loudly like clowns at the circus; and cars full of young people drive too fast; and things rattle and crash. But all the time there is an undercurrent. This is a town that knows what it is and where it's going. It is moving forward, it is expanding, and the young and the old know they are taking on the world and they are winning.*
>
> *'This is the best town in the world,' said a teenager I met outside the new Riddings Centre.*
>
> *As she moved on, into the concrete and glass structure that towered above us, blue and white in the sunshine, it was hard to disagree.*

### Task 9

Write down the most effective examples of:

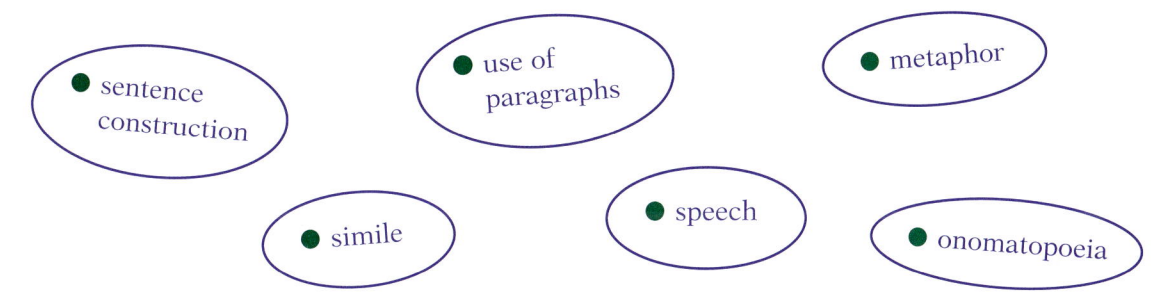

- sentence construction
- use of paragraphs
- metaphor
- simile
- speech
- onomatopoeia

Say what makes each example effective.

### Task 10

Write a few short paragraphs about an exciting place you know.
Imitate the style of the passage above.

**Examiner's Summary**

- Answer the question that has been set.
- Fulfil the Writing Process.
- Ensure you have a strong beginning and ending.
- Make the response interesting.
- Concentrate on vocabulary, sentence length and paragraphing.

Unit 13 Writing to Describe

# Unit 14 Final Revision for English

**Targets**
1. To be well prepared to answer both examination papers.
2. To focus on what is being tested.
3. To understand the skills required for success.

This unit deals with the period leading up to the exam, and 'last-minute' revision.

### Dealing with Paper 1, Section A

**1. Revise the technical vocabulary you need to answer the questions.**
Make sure you know:
- the meaning of each technical term (e.g. columns, subjective, rhetorical, etc.).
- the correct spellings
- how to use the words in sentences ('rhetoric' is the noun, 'rhetorical' the adjective).

**2. Read non-literary texts regularly.**
In each one find:
- facts
- opinions
- what the argument is saying.

Make notes on:
- audience and message
- layout/presentation
- language
- purpose.

**3. Write proper answers from your notes.**
Imagine there are 12 marks for the question and write your answer in 12 minutes. Make sure you quote from the text to prove your points.

**4. Think about using the hour for Section A effectively.**
Remember you must:
- read the texts carefully
- answer what is asked
- be guided by bullet points in the final question
- check how many marks are given for each question and divide up your time accordingly.

**Dealing with Paper 2, Section A**

**1** **Re-read regularly the poems you have studied.**
When you begin the examination paper you should:
- be able to choose immediately which poems to write about, because you know them so well
- not have to read the poems – just use them to find suitable quotations.

**2** **Improve your annotations.**
- Make sure you have only notes, not complete sentences.
- Rub out notes you no longer need.
- Replace them with more precise notes covering **meaning** and **poetic techniques** (similes, metaphors, rhyme, rhythm, etc.).
- Highlight important features, if that helps you.

Check you understand the poetic techniques you have been taught or have noted on your poems and how they make a poem more effective: e.g. an alliteration of 'd' sounds might give the impression of drumbeats.
Do not just spot the techniques – always explain their use in each case.

**Know Your Techniques**
**EXAMINER'S TIP!**

## PART 1 Poets

1. **Remember**
   You will:
   - have two questions on your poet, but should **answer only one**.
   - be asked about **two poems in each question**.

2. **Decide**
   which poems:
   - seem to 'go together': plan to write about them as a pair
   - you would most like to write about – if they 'come up' on the paper, you will be prepared for success.

3. **Write 30-minute practice answers**
   for each poetry pair, focusing on meanings and techniques.
   Write:
   - a brief introduction (3 minutes)
   - about each poem (12 minutes on each)
   - a brief conclusion (3 minutes).

4. **Think about what might be asked**
   Be prepared for:
   - unexpected questions or pairings, by knowing the poems well
   - bullet points: if they are offered, use them to guide your ideas
   - questions that expect more than simple meanings: you will be asked about the poems' messages, rather than the story; how the poet puts across a message; or differences between poems.

Unit 14 Final Revision for English

## PART 2

### Poems from Other Cultures and Traditions

Follow the guidelines offered for Poets.

In addition, remember **every** question will involve mention of other cultures and/or traditions. Make sure you are prepared for that 'angle'.

### Important Guidelines for Paper 2, Section A
You should:
- spend half an hour on each question
- answer the question set
- concentrate on one poem at a time:
  make comparisons as you write about the second one
- quote briefly
- analyse, do not just say what happens.

### Dealing with Paper 1 and Paper 2, Section B

**1 Revise approaches to the questions**
Make sure you know how to:
- use the Writing Process
- write to argue, persuade, instruct, inform, explain and describe
- use layouts appropriately, e.g. articles, leaflets, letters, etc.

If necessary, re-do Units from this book.

**2 Read any available material**
- See how the writing is structured.
- Notice how writers use technical effects, like sentence structure, similes and metaphors.
- Note down useful discourse markers ('moreover', 'as I have said', etc.).
- Practise short copies of different styles.

**3 Write short extracts to practise for each question**
For example, produce extracts from:
- a speech, **arguing** against your parents, that you should be allowed to stay out later
- a letter, to **persuade** your friend to lend you money
- **instructions** about driving a car
- a leaflet, **informing** teenagers about the dangers of drugs

## 3  Continued

- a statement to the police, in which you **explain** why your friend was leaving a shop with Cliff Richard's latest CD under his coat
- your autobiography, where you **describe** the happiest moment of your life.

## 4  Think about how to cope in the examination

Remember you will:
- select one question to answer
- plan, write and check
- pause every half page and ensure you are still answering the question
- use the time appropriately.

# Final Reminders

**Paper 1, Section A**
1. Answer all the questions set.
2. Underline on your question paper, if it helps.
3. Spend one minute per mark.
4. Answer all the bullet points.
5. Prove what you say.

**FOCUS**
Argue
Persuade
Instruct
Inform
Explain
Describe

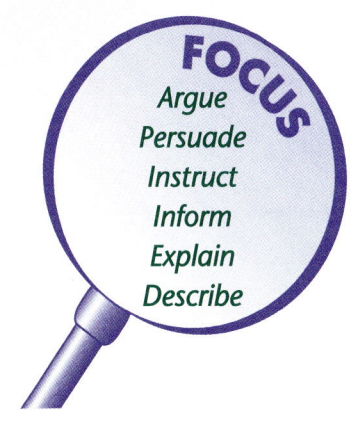

**Paper 2, Section A**
1. Answer only:
   - one question in each part
   - the question set.
2. Spend 30 minutes on each part.
3. Write about technique, not just the story.
4. Quote, but briefly.

**Section B Questions**
1. Choose one question.
2. Answer the question set.
3. Always use the Writing Process.
4. Spend:
   - 10 minutes planning
   - 40 minutes writing
   - 10 minutes checking.
5. Write two sides.

**Finally**
Enter the examination room properly prepared and you will feel in control. The skills in this book can help you to success: you have practised them – demonstrate them on the big day.
Examiners want to award good marks – give them the opportunity!

*Good Luck*

Unit 14  Final Revision for English

# Unit 15 Your Final Check List

Check through this list to see that you have covered all the necessary skills and revision areas. The right-hand column tells you which Unit you can go back to, where relevant, if you need to re-do or re-learn a skill.

| | YES | NO | GO TO UNIT |
|---|---|---|---|
| **Do you know?** | | | |
| • The date and time of each examination | | | – |
| • What each examination involves (e.g. how many papers, how long, etc.) | | | 1 & 14 |
| • For which examination you need to bring your Anthology | | | 1 & 14 |
| **Have you?** | | | |
| • Learnt how to divide up your time in the examination | | | 14 |
| • Read a range of non-literary material | | | 2 |
| • Noticed how it is presented | | | 3 |
| • Learnt to recognise fact and opinion and how they are used | | | 2 |
| • Learnt the technical vocabulary you will need in Paper 1, Section A | | | 4 |
| • Practised comparing texts, using bullet points to guide you | | | 3 |
| • Made notes in your Anthology for the poems you have studied | | | 14 |
| • Learnt the technical terms relating to poetry | | | – |
| • Decided which poems you would like to answer on | | | – |
| • Practised by answering likely questions on the poetry | | | – |
| **Can you ...?** | | | |
| • Write appropriately for different purposes and audiences | | | 6 |
| • Plan an essay quickly and effectively | | | 6 |
| • Put together a palette of appropriate words, phrases and discourse markers | | | 6 |
| • Argue effectively | | | 8 |
| • Persuade effectively | | | 9 |
| • Instruct effectively | | | 10 |
| • Inform clearly | | | 11 |
| • Explain precisely and effectively | | | 12 |
| • Describe, bringing your description to life | | | 13 |
| • Check and appropriately alter your writing | | | 6 |
| **Finally ...** | | | |
| • Do you know what makes the difference between one grade and another? | | | 2–13 |